COMMUNICATING WITH YOUR TEENAGER

Sheila Munro

Piccadilly Press • London

*Sheila Munro is a trainer and communication consultant.
She has worked in the field of parent support and education for
seven years, and has written and broadcast extensively on family
issues. She was born in Glasgow, lives in London
and is the parent of a teenage son.*

Designed by Clair Stutton
Printed and bound by WBC, Bridgend for the publishers
Piccadilly Press Ltd., 5 Castle Road, London NW1 8PR

A catalogue record for this book is available from
the British Library

ISBN: 1 85340 511 6

Cover design by Paul Cooper

ACKNOWLEDGEMENTS

Acknowledgement is due to Parent Network, the national charity that provides parenting education programmes, for its deep understanding of parents and parenting issues and, in particular, its course for parents of teenagers, where some of my learning took place.

I'd like to thank my son and his friends for providing advice and real-life examples of teenage issues. I'd also like to thank my mother and sister and friends and colleagues for their support and encouragement.

Thanks to Gerry Siperius for the poem, *It Has No Mercy*. And special thanks to all members of my 'Parents of Teenagers' support group: Sue, Barbara, Richard, Martin, Helen and Chrissie. See you in the caff.

S.R.M.

Other books in the How To Help Your Child series:

CONTENTS

FOREWORD

It seems a cruel trick of nature that, just when you think you've mastered the art of being a parent, your offspring hit puberty and turn from adorable little children into beautiful, yet hideous creatures – sometimes overnight. Driven by hormones, they may be prone to emotional outbursts, mood swings, depression and antisocial behaviour, and suddenly the communication skills and strategies you've carefully developed over the years no longer seem effective.

The purpose of this book is to help you build on skills you already have and develop new ones to cope with those sometimes turbulent adolescent years. If you feel the rug has been pulled from under your feet, it may help you replace it with different, more solid ground. I hope it enables you not only to cope, but also to enjoy your teenager as she or he progresses into young adulthood.

The focus of the book is not so much on solving problems as communicating about issues so that you and your teenager can work things out together. Communication itself is one of the greatest problem solvers. Please note: different things work for different people, and there is no guarantee that any of my suggestions will work for you. I hope that some of them do.

Chapter One
RELATIONSHIPS AND COMMUNICATION

COMMUNICATION IS THE KEY

Living with pre-teen or teenagers can be one of the most challenging times in parents' lives. Although not as physically demanding as looking after a young child, it can be mentally and emotionally, not to mention financially exhausting. Just when we're relieved to see that our children seem well-adjusted and are becoming more independent, they lurch into major changes that can seriously affect their behaviour and attitude. Good-natured, balanced children can metamorphose into rude, tempestuous adolescents. Then, just when we are at our wits' end, they may change again into charming and sensible young people.

Most young people *are* sensible and aware. But even the most 'aware' teenagers are likely to start asserting their will and testing existing rules and values – and we, as parents, are the obvious testing board. As we watch them change shape – sometimes in front of our very eyes – their relationships with us, with themselves and with others change shape as well. Communication under these circumstances can be difficult and often painful. But taking the time and trouble to communicate effectively can be a real invest-ment. It can save a lot of time, and possibly trouble, later.

If the communication isn't working, try changing your way of communicating. You'll find ways of doing that in this book. Even a minor adjustment in communication can have a beneficial effect on your teenager and his or her response. Focusing on the *way* we communicate is more likely to change things for the better than putting all our attention on the teenager. Communication is not only the key to enhancing the relationship between parent and teenager: it *is* the relationship. It is the substance of everyday contact, which is often the most exasperating thing of all. Improving the quality of our communication can make the difference not only to everyday interactions but also between dreading our teenagers and daring to enjoy them.

WE'VE ALL BEEN TEENAGERS

One way of helping our relationship with our teenager is to recall our own experiences at that age and to remember how it feels to be a teenager. Remembering some of the highs and lows of our own adolescence helps us to be more understanding of the moods and needs of our teenager. However, resist the temptation to say, 'When I was your age . . .' , which is guaranteed to raise a yawn. Whatever lesson of life *you* may have learned, teenagers have to discover it for themselves anyway. For you, being a teenager may be history; for them it is the first time a human being has ever had to endure whatever it is they're going through.

Your relationship with your own parents may still be affecting you now. For example, the chances are that if they were very strict with you, you probably compensated by going the other way with your own children, perhaps being over-lenient with them – or vice versa. There is, of course, no golden rule, but if you want to change patterns of communication with your teenager, it helps to understand where you learned your own patterns of communicating.

One thing is sure: our offspring, at whatever age trigger memories of and reactions to our own experiences at the same age. Feelings and incidents buried deep down can return to the surface and cloud the waters of the present situation with our child or teenager. If you went through a very troubled adolescence yourself, or still feel unresolved about particular incidents and/or suffered abuse or other trauma, it may be prudent to seek professional help from a therapist or counsellor. (See 'Useful Addresses', page 141.) Recovering from our own hurts can help us be more available and open to our teenagers.

TIMES HAVE CHANGED

The main difference between then and now is that you're the grown-up now. You are probably facing the challenge of approaching middle age while your youngster is hurtling towards the full fountain of youth. Just as trees sprout leaves, so adolescents undergo big changes. Some things are universal. But society itself is changing constantly, and the conditions in which parents and teenagers are living now are quite different from two or three generations ago.

For parents, life is more complex. No one needs to have spelled out the pressures of balancing work and family life. If you're working full time, you're probably working long hours that leave precious little time for household chores, let alone time with your children or partner, if you have one. If you're working part time, you may have two or even three part-time jobs on different days of the week or evenings. You may have children of different ages at different schools in different areas, requiring you to ferry them around each day (school transport being a rarity nowadays). If you're unemployed, you may have more time on your hands but are almost certainly enduring financial hardship. In the economic realities of the present day, there is a serious imbalance between money and time.

For teenagers, too, life is complex. Through the media teenagers are more exposed than ever before to all kinds of information and influences. This can make parents feel as though they're having to compete to make their voices heard. However, the positive effect is that teenagers nowadays tend to be more worldly-wise, aware of many global, political and ecological issues. Consequently, they are less likely to have the wool pulled over their eyes or listen unquestioningly to those in authority, which includes you. Young people now are also more aware of their rights.

THE ROLE OF A PARENT

Obviously, our role as a parent changes as our child develops. Yet it's surprising how many parents attempt to cling to an inappropriate parenting role that has long been outgrown by the child. That's not to say that they still attempt to spoonfeed their teenagers but, on an emotional level, they may still see themselves as being in a position of control. This is helpful neither for themselves nor their teenager. It is more useful for parents to help their teenagers make their own decisions and look after themselves more.

Of course, letting go of control can be hard, especially when we know our teenager is still a long way from being a mature adult. We need to be able to balance our response. But if we cling to our teenagers they'll pull away harder, and if we push them too soon they'll cling. This is where the role of the parent is crucial: not letting go of the reins abruptly, but gradually giving more responsibility and allowing more independence until she or he is ready to move on to the next stage. The whole process takes years – in fact, you've probably been doing it very skilfully ever since they were little, letting them climb a gate or take their first ride down a slide. What's harder when they're teenagers is that the risks seem greater – they're out in the big, bad world now, and although old enough to make their own decisions, these may not always be the right decisions – and because they're bigger people they have further to fall.

It's important to remember that you still have a role to play. Because teenagers are learning about responsibility, they need lots of practice. It's as if they're still wearing L-plates (learning to be adults) and you are their coach, supporting rather than instructing them. You are also still in the indispensable role of giving them something to push against, and eventually pull away from, which every teenager needs.

THE ROLE OF A TEENAGER

While the sole activities of a teenager might sometimes appear to be to sleep, loll about at home, and go out and have fun with friends, such activities may have a serious side as well. A teenager's job is to break away, break out and learn how to be an adult. From our point of view, 'learning to be an adult' may be about taking responsibility; from theirs, it may be more about having fun and freedom, romance and sex. They have to develop on many levels. These include emotional, mental and social as well as physical development. (And some development happens in their sleep.)

Often their role is to test and possibly reject existing social, spiritual and family values and rediscover life anew. They are taking their first deep breaths of adult life, and sometimes this can be intoxicating. It can also be a confusing and deeply distressing time. External self-consciousness can be made worse by internal angst. The great quest for identity – 'Who am I?' – is part of the process of becoming an adult. This also explains the many different fashions and phases a lot of young people go through during the teenage years.

Sadly, just as you may increasingly see their flaws and imperfections, so do they, too, see your imperfections. It is as if nature is lifting a veil to release you psychologically as well as physically from one another. As your son or daughter emerges from the seemingly cosy state of childhood, you, too, are obliged to let slip the rosy-tinted spectacles. This can leave you (and them) feeling very raw – a bit like waking up to cold reality at the end of a relationship when all the magic has gone – each realising that both you, and they, are not such nice people after all. Which of course has its rewards as well. OK, so they're not perfect and neither are you – isn't that liberating?

They are constantly changing, and constantly challenging your views. *This is what they're programmed to do.* So it's important not to take it all too personally, even though a lot of their challenging and testing may be directed at you. If this is a problem, try being a bit more detached. After all, if they were someone else's teenagers, you probably wouldn't feel half so bothered by their views and would probably even enjoy a stimulating debate with them. And if they make us question our own beliefs and values, they can help keep us open-minded and young. (Tell yourself that next time you're feeling very, very old.)

THE ROLE OF THE PEER GROUP

As your son or daughter progresses into the teenage years, she or he will probably have a group of friends with whom she or he 'hangs out' whenever possible. These friends are often of the same gender. Whether the group is made up of just one or two friends (as is likely with girls) or a larger group (more common with boys), this peer group is important for many reasons.

Not only does the group help its members develop social skills, but it also plays a major part in helping a young person make the transition from the safety of the family into the outside world. In the natural process of moving away, the adolescent is 'growing out' of the family and needs something to take its place. The peer group offers a different kind of group, one that offers protection and support from friends rather than family. It helps a young person learn about being interdependent as well as independent.

Peer groups can sometimes seem threatening to parents, partly because – however good a bunch your child's friends may seem to be – you know instinctively they are beginning to replace the family as the centre of his or her world. If you don't know your child's friends, or if you suspect they are up to violent or criminal behaviour, the group can be much more threatening. Make it your business to know who your son's or daughter's friends are and what they are up to. The best way to meet them is to welcome them into your home, if you haven't already done so. But if you have serious concerns, talk about them with your teenager. Remember that, though you may be unable to influence the group, you can still have a strong influence at home. If things seem to be getting too much out of hand, you may even have to encourage your teenager to hang out with a different crowd, and pro-vide opportunities for her or him to make new friends.

Later, as they become older teenagers, they become more independent and grow out of the peer group, to seek more intimate, one-to-one relationships.

POWER-SHIFTS WITHIN THE FAMILY

Often our children hit adolescence before we've even

thought about it. We may have felt the odd tremor, felt the earth rumbling under our feet, then one day find ourselves in the middle of a full-blown earthquake.

This, of course, can be very distressing, having our familiar world turned upside-down, and can leave us feeling fearful and powerless. For we sense we *are* losing power while experiencing our son or daughter as increasingly more powerful. One of the biggest sources of conflict between parents and teenagers is the struggle for control and power. Just as a young person grows in size and stature, she or he separates more from parental authority and grows in status and authority as well. As a consequence, the entire base of power and authority in the household is shifting. Parents have to be willing to relinquish some of their own authority to make room for the new, emerging authority. If a parent tries to hold on to all the authority at this stage, this will almost certainly be challenged. If, on the other hand, the parent lets go of authority too soon, the adolescent will almost certainly take over. Most of us know at least one household where it is the teenager who rules the roost.

These dynamics affect other members of the family and can lead to quite an unsettled situation. Because the basis of the relationship is changing, parents may sometimes feel as if the rug has been pulled from under their feet. Learning to share power is a challenge for any parent, especially if she or he feels that the teenager is not ready or responsible enough – or, the teenager may not even want to take it. But if we work at finding a new balance and help our teenagers learn to *handle* responsibility and power, we may find a different way of relating at a deeper, firmer level. If the original ground underneath was shaky already, however – for example, in the case of adoptive or foster-parents – this may be a time of extra turbulence, and you may well be advised to be kind to yourselves and seek outside help. (See 'Useful Addresses', page 141.)

Part of the push-pull struggle also comes from tension within ourselves: part of us emotionally wanting to separate and push our children away, wanting them to grow up, and part of us wanting to hold on, not really wanting to let go. Here are two suggestions for helping to manage the whole process:

- As a parent, *you still have power, and it's important to use it.* If you use your authority wisely and well, you are setting an example for your teenager to follow and helping her or him learn how to use her or his own authority.
- Whatever the family dynamics, and however obnoxious or difficult the teenager's behaviour, *avoid making the teenager a scapegoat.* That is, avoid making the person the problem and concentrate instead on what it is about the *behaviour* that is a problem. (More about this in Chapter Three.)

   Above all, if you are experiencing difficulties with your teenager, try to focus on the *relationship* between you rather than putting all the attention on her or him. Even when things are going well, the more you do this the more you will help to prevent major crises occurring. Living with a teenager can be nerve-racking; when we succeed in communicating, it can be exhilarating as well.

Chapter Two
EASING THE PRESSURE

In order to make communication easier, it helps to look at what is making it difficult. Just acknowledging some of the pressures that we and our teenagers face can help take some of the pressure off communication itself. Addressing some of these pressures may help give both us, and our teenagers, an easier time.

PRESSURES ON TEENAGERS

Teenagers are undergoing their own pressures of growth and change. At the same time there is the stress of school (including the change from primary to secondary school), tests, homework and exams. In addition, there is more pressure than ever before to grow up sooner (partly caused by other pressures in society – see 'Pressures on Parents', page 25), and in many instances teenagers seem expected to have girl-friends or boyfriends and behave like young adults almost before they have made the transition from childhood. In addition:

- There are pressures from advertising, often targeted at teenagers, to smoke this, drink that, wear this, and have a particular image or body shape. At the same time, ironically, the media often gives adolescents (boys particularly) bad press. Commercialism also raises material expectations that are often unrealistic against a backdrop of poverty and high unemployment. It is often the 'victims' of commercialism who serve to promote it: in other words, peer pressure seriously adds to the commercial pressures.

- Parents, too, can put pressures on their teenager to achieve academically or otherwise or to form girlfriend-boyfriend relationships too soon. Or they may give their teenager too much responsibility too soon, expecting too much support or expecting him or her to be self-sufficient. They may expect him or her to be emotionally mature and behave like an adult before he or she is ready to do so. Remember that every individual is different: there are early developers and late developers and a whole range in between. To help teenagers realise their full potential, it's vital to allow them to develop at their own pace. They have enough other pressures to contend with.
- Teenagers are also faced with the pressures of making career choices and deciding subject options at school. At the same time, the eternal question 'What do you want to *be*?' is increasingly redundant as most of us now understand that a job is not necessarily a job for life any more. Our offspring are likely to go through several changes in career and employment status in their lives, and helping them learn how to be flexible, resourceful

and adaptable may be one of the greatest gifts they receive from you.

• There is nothing new, of course, in the association of teenagers with 'sex, drugs and rock-'n'-roll' – except it's different music now.

SEX

As well as the natural, internal pressures (the 'got-a-rocket-in-my-pocket' syndrome), there is often intense social pressure on young people to be sexually active before they're ready to be. Sex is everywhere, from posters to TV.

You can help your teenager by discussing these pressures and by making him or her aware that in any situation there are choices, and helping him or her feel confident in making choices that are right for him or her. This independence of mind can apply to any situation – not just in matters relating to sex. For example, if your teenager seems unsure whether or not to go out with a particular friend, you could try asking 'What feels right for you?'

It's never too soon for them to know about contraception and AIDS, so that when they are ready for sex, they are prepared. Some parents are afraid that if they broach the subject they may be condoning or encouraging their teenagers in being sexually active, but sometimes *not* communicating can be a way of colluding with a particular situation. Obviously, *when* and *how* you broach the subject do matter. You can talk to your children about sex or give them a book about it, explaining that the chat or the book is for them to learn from, not because you want them to start having sex.

With the risks associated with sexually transmitted diseases like AIDS, it is vital that your teenager has a sensible understanding of the issues. And it is your responsibility as a parent to be aware of the facts yourself so that you can communicate with your teenager about these issues. If you're worried that you don't know enough, it is important that you educate yourself – for example, by obtaining literature from the many agencies and charities offering their services. (See 'Useful Addresses', page 141.) As well as allaying any irrational fears, such literature will enable you to give accurate information to your child. (If you *don't* know what you're talking about, they are unlikely to take you seriously.)

Today's teenager is often extremely wordly-wise and may already know a lot more about these subjects than you do, which is why it is wise to discuss sex with them before they are teenagers and then discuss sexually related issues as they arise in conversation, in the news, or wherever.

DRUGS

There are more pressures on teenagers than ever before to take drugs. This is partly due to a much more accessible drugs market, with its own methods of advertising and marketing. While our parents may have despaired of our smoking dope, today's parents are faced with an increased array of recreational and hard drugs to worry about their teenagers having access to. However, exhorting young people to 'just say no' isn't helpful. Research has proved that the 'just say no' approach was not an effective campaign.

Again, teenagers need to be well-informed of the effects as well as the risks of different drugs so that they can make their own informed choices. If you as a parent have clear facts, this will enable you to convey a balanced view and discuss the issues with your teenager, which can have a more beneficial effect on the young person than fearful scaremongering. Telling someone he or she will die if he or she takes a particular drug, for example, is as bad as the Victorians saying people would go blind if they masturbated. (And did it stop them? is the question.) Also, if you overreact, teenagers won't respect your opinions and may not listen to *anything* you say.

Above all, it's important to keep the drugs issue in perspective.

Recently, a mother of young children confided that although she was enjoying her children at this young age she was terrified of when they become teenagers. 'There are just so many dangers nowadays,' she said, 'especially with all the drugs.' These words were spoken through a haze of tobacco smoke and against the clinking of a glass of a large gin and tonic.

There is nothing new in alcohol and yet it still has the highest addiction rate. We also know that tobacco damages health. Both tobacco and alcohol are very real threats to teenagers. If we put more energy into looking at our own addictive tendencies (including addictions to legal, pharmaceutical drugs) we would set more of an example to young people than expecting them to set an example to us. Fortunately, in spite of tobacco advertising specifically targeting young people, many teenagers know it's cool *not* to smoke. Many adults believe we need to relinquish the hold tobacco has on our society before we can effectively debate whether or not cannabis should be legalised. Cannabis has already become part of mainstream smoking culture.

If you are worried that your son or daughter may have a problem with drug or alcohol abuse, contact one of the agencies specialising in guidance and support.

CLUBS AND RAVES

Licensed clubs are meant to admit only people aged eighteen and over, though many teenagers lie about their age to gain admittance. All-night raves may or may not have a licence, depending on who has organised them. Although anarchic and enjoyable affairs for teenagers, parents are advised to think very carefully about letting an underage teenager go to one unless accompanied by a responsible adult.

In all these circumstances, if you are worried about what your teenager has been getting up to, it helps to ask about her or his experiences *in an interested way.* Asking 'What was that like?' has a very different feel from 'Why did you do that?' 'Why' is an accusatory word, almost guaranteed to put her or him on the defensive. Giving an opportunity to talk about experiences in a friendly rather than blameful way may help him or her make positive choices in the future.

SAFETY

Violence and crime have been on the increase, often related to drug and alcohol abuse. Not surprisingly, many parents fear for their children's safety. While young women are more at risk of sexual attack, young men are more at risk of violence from other males. It's vital to instil awareness of safety in your child (preferably before he or she becomes a teenager) so that he or she avoids, where possible, putting him- or herself at risk. Obvious examples are ensuring that they know about the dangers of drink-driving (including being a passenger) and of being out on their own late at night.

There is no doubt that the world can be a dangerous place. The best protection of all is a young person's common sense and awareness that she or he is capable of making careful decisions about his or her safety. A way of encouraging this is to gradually give your teenager more responsibility, *with support*, for making decisions.

At the end of the day it is important to keep the safety issue in perspective and to remember that young people are more at risk from road accidents than from 'stranger danger'. They need training from an early age in road safety as well as learning about being streetwise. And, most importantly, you need to make them not afraid but aware.

PRESSURES ON PARENTS

Chapter One looked at financial pressures, the pressures of employment and unemployment, and the difficulties of balancing work and family life. In addition:

- Family structures themselves have been changing. Families tend to be smaller, with fewer brothers and sisters to interact, thus putting more onus on the parents. Many of us are in one-parent families or step-families as a result of separation and divorce. These family situations can be liberating and rewarding; they can also bring complex problems that our parents may not have had to deal with. 'Inventing the wheel', with no example to follow, can be hard work.

  Changing family structures result also in an increase of absent or part-time parents, which itself brings a range of complicated issues.

- In our diverse society, we may be bringing up our children with cultural traditions and beliefs which are different from those of our next-door neighbours. Living in a multicultural world can be exciting; it can also be challenging. You may belong to an oppressed minority in society, struggling to maintain your culture, language and values, and to help your teenager overcome discrimination.

- Families have become 'closed' and more isolated. Communities are more fragmented, with less support for parents. Few of us live close to our own parents any more, and relationships with other family members are harder to sustain because of distance. This means that elders and other relatives are often absent from everyday family life and also that the benefits of the extended family have been lost. With fewer cousins and grandparents and uncles and aunts around, a teenage member of the family has fewer people to relate to and more responsibility falls on the parents.

Feelings of isolation can also increase for parents when a child makes the transition to secondary school, and there is no longer the chance to meet other parents at the school gates, for example.

- The role of fathers and mothers has changed from the traditional and stereotypical roles of our parents' time, with many more women as bread-winners and more men taking actively caring roles. Many of these roles are interchangeable between couples, bringing greater freedom and flexibility. However, such a scenario can also make more work for both parents and can itself be a cause of tension.

With all these pressures, it is no wonder that many parents nowadays feel stressed. In addition, you may be coping with ill health in the family, or you or your child may be disabled, bringing another set of challenges.

Yet there is still very little support for or recognition of the valuable work parents perform in society. (Except when things go wrong, when parents are blamed instantly.) Instead, parents tend to be full of internal pressures – blaming ourselves with feelings of guilt or inadequacy at having 'failed' in some way. If this applies to you, stop right there. Let yourself off the hook and go out and celebrate the magnificent job you've done so far!

COMMUNICATION REVOLUTION?

Since they were children, our adolescents have grown up in a high-tech world. Now, as well as phones and televisions, video recorders, satellites and computers, there are mobile phones, the Internet and digital broadcasting. Many parents enjoy the world of computers with their children and teenagers; others feel left behind, unskilled and unfamiliar with the language. If you are one of these parents, there are many books and user-friendly computer courses for beginners – if you want to learn, that is.

TEENAGERS AND PHONES

Telephones still feature high on the technological list. Sometimes it may seem as if your teenager conducts her or his entire social life over the phone, or at least occupies the wires for a large part of her or his time. This monopoly may make it hard for other family members to get a look- (or rather listen-) in. Discuss this with your teenager and agree a time-limit if necessary. If they spend over a certain amount, the excess could be deducted from pocket money. It may be worthwhile investing in a second line if you haven't already done so, and negotiating a deal over the phone bill. In cases of serious telephone abuse, consider putting a lock on the phone.

Accepting the role of telephones in our teenager's life, however, may help to take some of the heat out of the situation. Telephones help sustain social and emotional development by giving:

- the opportunity to practise telephone skills, and

- the chance to hold intimate conversations that may not be possible in other situations, such as at school.

Phones are sometimes a substitute for or a way of staying in contact with the peer group, especially when friends may live a distance from one another, making it impractical to hang around the street corner together.

Telephones can also be a good way for us to keep in touch with our teenagers. If we instil good habits early on (preferably before they're teenagers), they will know to phone or leave notes and let you know where they are, who they are with and when they expect to be home. The best way to do this is to set an example yourself by phoning home or leaving notes when *you* go out, letting them know where you are and how you may be contacted, etc. By doing so you are taking equal responsibility. (It may be useful to let them have a charge card, too.)

EVOLUTION, NOT REVOLUTION

For all the technical advances, at times person-to-person communication may seem to have regressed – especially when, say, you have an adolescent who communicates in monosyllables and grunts (not an uncommon phenomenon for someone who, moments earlier, was being highly articulate on the telephone). To be fair, though, it isn't only adolescents but the whole of society which still has a long way to go in terms of person-to-person communication. We only need to look at the state of the world and the conflicts in our own relationships and community to know that this is so. For most of us there is room for progress.

Developing our interpersonal communication skills can have every bit as powerful an effect on our everyday lives as any technical advances. Doing so may even revolutionise the relationship with our teenager.

RITES AND RITUALS

Some of the things that have been lost in the industrial technoculture are rituals and ceremonies for rites of passage in the human life cycle. Of course, many religious ceremonies are still performed, such as christenings, Bar Mitzvahs, marriages and burial rites. But whereas nowadays, for instance, a mother may say 'Take an aspirin, dear' to a daughter who is starting her first period, in traditional (and some existing) cultures there would be a celebration with other women of the community to mark the girl's transition into womanhood. For boys, it might have been an initiation into the men's circle after their first blood-letting in battle. (Significantly, there is still a fascination for this, especially among young men, although their participation is reduced to watching such scenes on TV or video – which raises the question: do violent technomovies help *prevent* violence?

The point of these rituals and ceremonies was that they were collective communication, community events that helped to *contain* change as well as celebrate it. Without them, the young people and parents are left on their own with the change, with all the stress of managing it but without the fun or support of others.

Of course, there are ways of creating one's own

rituals, and parties can be as good a ritual as any. Young people are good at spontaneously creating their own celebrations. Mothers can help welcome their daughter into a women's 'circle', and fathers can play an active role in including their sons in men-only events: for example, going on a long hike or taking them to the most common ritual of all, football. (Please note: although many women enjoy football as well, I am talking here about gender-specific initiations, without being stereotypical.)

ATMOSPHERE

Communication is made easier in a convivial rather than a fraught atmosphere. At times, of course, this is absolutely not possible, and sometimes very powerful communication happens in moments of tension. However, to set up a *habit* of positive communication in the family, it is helpful to create certain conditions, for example:

- slow down sometimes; take time out from all the hurly-burly;
- switch off the TV sometimes; spend time quietly together, in the same room, even if you're not talking;
- eat together when possible (another ritual) and talk while you eat;
- encourage discussion of all kinds of issues, and
- do chores together sometimes and talk 'sideways' (in the same way that a ride in a car sometimes can create the time and space in which to communicate).

ATTITUDE

However much we improve our communication skills, the techniques and skills by themselves are worth nothing without the basis of a healthy attitude. In fact, it could almost be said that *attitude is all*. Our attitude comes across in any communication with our teenager. Some positive pointers about attitude are:

- *Keep problems in perspective.* The fact that he or she hasn't done his or her chores today isn't necessarily going to affect how he or she turns out as an adult.
- *Be willing to help.* However obnoxious or difficult their behaviour, teenagers still need help sometimes and you are often the best person to give it.
- *Be willing and able to listen.* Listening to your teenager will convey an open and supportive rather than a punitive or dismissive attitude. (Listening is different from giving advice, which they may not take anyway.) Being listened to helps a teenager feel valued, and a teenager who feels valued is more likely to value himself or herself as well as others.
- *Talk to your teenager as you would to another adult* – that is, with interest and respect.
- *Be open to negotiation.* Discuss issues such as pocket money and negotiate a deal, including household chores, for example. This can apply to many situations with your teenager and can be very satisfying if you reach an agreement that works for both of you.
- *Be accepting of your teenager.* This doesn't mean *agreeing* with her or him or condoning certain

behaviour – just because you accept the person doesn't mean you accept the behaviour. It means taking him or her exactly as she or he is, at any moment, *without judging*. Many teenagers say they feel on trial.

- *Avoid having unrealistic expectations.* Of course we all want our teenagers to grow into fulfilled, competent and caring adults. But do you have over-high expectations of them? Are you expecting them to grow into perfect human beings? Placing too many demands can create pressure that can cramp rather than enhance their style. The one thing you can reasonably expect is that, whatever issues she or he is grappling with right now, she or he will probably 'turn out all right' in the end.

- *Give positive not negative attention* – for example, instead of giving attention to negative behaviour, noticing and showing approval of positive behaviour or of a *change* of behaviour. Giving too much attention to negative behaviour often serves only to reinforce that behaviour, especially if the behaviour is attention-seeking in the first place.

- *Be accepting of yourself.* You are probably doing the best you can (and you're not perfect, either). Many of us are afraid of being judged by others on the appearance and behaviour of our children and teenagers. (Teenagers are often more visible.) If you feel guilty or inadequate as a parent, then it's time to change your negative thought patterns about yourself.

- *Be real.* If you're in debt, or going through difficulties at work or in your relationship, it's better to bring matters into the open than pretend that everything's fine when it isn't. This doesn't mean burdening your teenager inappropriately with all the details or all your problems; it means being honest about what is going on for you. That way your teenager grows up understanding some of the complex problems in life and how to go about resolving them.

A teenager who is over-shielded from the tougher side of life may have a bit of a shock coming to her or him and may find it harder to cope, eventually, as an adult.

- *Be relaxed.* This is not to say be completely laid back and passive; nor is it saying don't express your feelings; it means being in a calm space to communicate and 'meet' the challenges of your teenager. We all know that when we are tense conflict is more likely to escalate. A good example is driving: if you're driving in traffic and you're in a calm state of mind, you're more likely to respond calmly to the erratic behaviour of other drivers, whereas if you're feeling tense, you're more likely to be provoked and overreact.

- *Keep your sense of humour.* Sometimes we can take ourselves a bit too seriously; it's good to be able to step back and have a good laugh (even if it's through the tears).

DEMONSTRATING ATTITUDE
The attitude behind every communication affects not only our communication but how it is received. Young people (including young children) can easily pick up

where we are coming from. The attitude *is* the communication.

If, for example, you are disapproving of your teenager, she or he will almost certainly sense this, even if you don't utter a single word. Then, when and if you speak, the communication will probably have already got off to a bad start. If, however, you consciously change your attitude, this will affect what you say and how it is received. Here is an example:

MOTHER (*frowning*): 'Your hair looks a mess.'
TEENAGER: 'You always say that. Anyway, it's my hair and I can dye it any colour I want to.'
MOTHER (*shouts*): 'Yes, but you're going to get into trouble at school now, and what will the neighbours say?'
TEENAGER: 'You're just boring and old-fashioned and I *hate* you.' (*goes out, slamming door*)

In the next example, the mother has changed her attitude from disapproval to impartiality. She doesn't like the colour of her son's hair, but recognises that *he's* the one who has to live with it:

MOTHER: 'You've dyed your hair!'
TEENAGER: 'Yeah, do you like it?'
MOTHER: 'No, actually, I don't. It's a bit over-the-top, isn't it?'
TEENAGER: 'Don't worry, Mum. You'll get used to it. I didn't expect you to like it, anyway.'

Note: the occasional bit of disapproval is healthy and

necessary sometimes: it can check different kinds of behaviour as well as giving teenagers street cred from being disapproved of by their parents, occasionally, in front of their friends. It is a *constant* attitude of disapproval which can be harmful. If you are aware of this in yourself, practise seeing your teenager as someone who is becoming more and more responsible rather than someone who is useless and incapable or who should like or do the things *you* would like them to. ('Responsible' here means capable of making their own decisions and has nothing to do with what colour they may decide to dye their hair.)

NON-VERBAL COMMUNICATION

Communication is more than talking and listening. We've looked at how behaviour and attitude can communicate deep, underlying messages. In addition, body language emits strong signals that can give a very accurate picture of what's going on. Often, unspoken messages have the most impact: as in the words of the old newspaper saying, 'A picture is worth more than a thousand words'.

Body language includes posture, gestures, tone of voice and facial expressions. Even if our youngsters are unforthcoming with verbal information, their body language can give a lot away. A hunched posture says 'Poor me, I'm feeling needy and/or sad and/or inadequate.' Hands on hips is a defiant pose, whereas crossed arms or legs suggest defensiveness. Think of the classic gangly young adolescent who is all arms and legs – his or her physical awkwardness or lack of physical coordination may reflect their inner state. Their various levels of development (mental, emotional, sexual) may be at completely different stages – hence the expression 'all over the place', meaning the whole person is generally 'out of synch'.

It has also been said that 'the body never lies'. Our own body language can be very revealing. In our communication, most of us are already unconsciously reading and responding to each other's body language as well as to spoken communication. (Just watch any two people in conversation to notice this.) We may try to hide a meaning, but our expression or tone may give us away: 'Yes, I'm willing to negotiate,' you might say, with your arms firmly folded. Young children are especially good at picking up mixed messages – that is, if we say one thing and mean another. A classic example of this is, 'No, you can't have any sweets', said with an apologetic smile that means 'Part of me wishes that you could, though'. An ensuing drama in the shop is guaranteed, with the child responding to the truth of the gesture rather than to the contradictory words.

To be effective in our communication with our teenager, we need to take care that we are communicating with congruence – that is, *saying what we mean* and ensuring that words and body are saying the same thing. For example, saying 'No' and clearly meaning it, or fully listening, facing the other person and sitting or standing at the same level rather than saying 'I'm listening' while turning away to do something else.

Also, it helps to be aware of what we're *feeling* at any time because feelings, too, communicate themselves in a powerful way. If we are not conscious of a particular emotion, such as anger or fear, that feeling is likely to leak out anyway through our body language and behaviour. So, for clear, assertive communication, it is important for our feelings, meanings and words to be fully integrated so that the power of our message flows unimpeded: for example, 'I feel furious that you've left a mess in the kitchen when you said you'd clear it up,' rather than saying with a forced smile, 'You still haven't done the washing up.'

Sometimes we can be of most support to our teenagers when we are just quiet and listen. Sometimes just being there is enough, communicating without words that we are available to listen if they want us to and without being intrusive. Remember:

COMMUNICATION IS MORE THAN WORDS
WORDS ARE MORE THAN TALKING
TALKING WITHOUT LISTENING IS ONE-WAY COMMUNICATION

THE POWER OF WORDS

Words have immense power. Many of our deepest inner wounds are caused by hurtful things that people have said to us. Words uttered by our own parents, teachers, friends, relatives, partner or lover may all have left their mark. Or our self-esteem may have been eroded as children by constant criticism.

Words also have the power to heal. They can have a positive effect in all kinds of situations; they can soothe troubles, calm storms; they have been demonstrated throughout time and tale to have magical powers.

There is no mystery, however, in the following guide to spoken communication with your teenager:

- *Avoid criticism.* Obviously, there is a place for *constructive* criticism, sometimes, but negative criticism wears down self-esteem and undermines confidence. If you are for ever 'on the back' of your teenager, you may be doing more damage than you realise. In fact, it could be said that

CRITICISM SERIOUSLY DAMAGES HEALTH

Mental and emotional health can be affected, and as a consequence physical health as well. A teenager who is criticised constantly is likely to feel unvalued and unsupported. This can lead to depression and/or antisocial behaviour, and the relationship between you and him or her will probably deteriorate. Before you despair, however, rest assured that this is something many (if not the majority of) parents do without thinking. But becoming *conscious* of our patterns helps us to start changing them. Just being aware of how we're communicating can make a difference, both in what we say and how our teenagers respond.

It can be hard not to criticise if *we* are being criticised by our teenager. However, if we break the pattern it may help them to do so as well. Giving up criticism doesn't mean being all-accepting or uncritical. It is *habitual* criticism that is harmful.

- *Give constructive criticism.* Try to be discerning in your criticism. This will have a more positive effect than if you criticise all the time. Learn the art of giving *feedback* (anyway, it sounds better than criticism). You can even ask, 'Do you mind if I give you some feedback?' This gives your teenager a choice – to say yes or no. (If the answer is no, respect that.) When you give feedback, always start your sentence with 'I' rather than 'You': for example, 'I notice when you put the rubbish out that you often leave a trail of plastic wrappers behind you,' rather than, 'You always make a terrible mess when you put the rubbish out.' This gives the teenager the opportunity to reply, 'Well, that's because the bag's too full and I can't tie it up.' It also gives a chance for you to discuss it:

PARENT: 'What would make a difference?'
TEENAGER: 'Empty it sooner, I suppose, before it got so full.'

Try to remain calm if you don't get the answer you'd like to have, and keep the lines of communication open.

By asking an open question – that is, one that doesn't require just a 'yes' or 'no' answer – the parent has helped the teenager come up with his or her own solution. Remember to give feedback on behaviour you *approve* of as well as behaviour you find difficult. Just saying 'I like the way you cook spaghetti/feed the cat/put the rubbish out on time/paint your nails' can work wonders at raising your teenager's self-esteem.

- *Avoid labels*. Labels are what we stick on jars of marmalade; they're also what we put on any person we may call 'stupid' or 'useless' or 'scruffy', and so on. These are labels that stick, especially if used often. They become internalised. It can be hard for a teenager to change once she or he has been labelled as something. Someone who is always called 'clumsy' will find it hard *not* to behave clumsily in the end. Much more helpful is to give a description of what has happened – 'Oops, you've dropped it,' or (rather than 'stupid') 'You don't find map-reading easy, do you? Would you like some help?'

- *Use positive language.* This doesn't mean never say no; it means using words that empower instead of words that have limitations. For example, saying 'should' can be very limiting. 'You should tidy your room' sounds like an order or a duty, whereas substituting the word 'could' offers more choice: 'You could tidy your room' sounds more of an option. Teenagers like to feel they have a choice, because then they can exert their own authority. (They may not tidy their room but at least they will feel better.) Ultimately, this can help them learn to be more responsible: if they then tidy their room they are doing so because they *choose* to, not because someone is making them.

Words like 'never' and 'always' can also be limiting. 'You never eat enough' or 'You're always late' leave no room for anything else and can be self-prophesying. Words like 'sometimes' or 'often' are more positive and leave the door open for communication.

Words can help to convey a positive message rather than a fearful one. For example, when a teenager is going out for the evening, saying 'Keep safe' is more empowering than 'Don't get into any trouble', helping to create a positive picture rather than a negative one.

- *Talk things through.* If issues have to be dealt with between you and your teenager, talk things through wherever possible. This sometimes means distancing yourself from a situation – that is, taking time to talk about it *after* the event, or away from the heat of the moment, when you are both calmer.

TRUSTING OUR INTUITION

Sometimes our intuition tells us something, but we don't necessarily take heed of it. My advice is: listen to your intuition. It may not always be accurate, but often it gives important signals that we might not otherwise receive. For example, we might say to our teenage daughter, 'Yes, of course you can go to the disco,' then have an intuition that that is not actually where she's going. The important thing, always, whatever the message, is to *check it out*. For example, say, 'I'm worried you intend going somewhere else instead of the disco,' but *not* 'You liar, I don't believe you.'

DAUGHTER: 'Don't worry, Mum, I'll be fine.'
MOTHER: 'Yes, but where are you going?'
DAUGHTER: 'To the disco. I told you. Then we're going to Nathan's. He's having a party.'
MOTHER: 'Well, you didn't tell me *that* before.'
DAUGHTER: 'Well, I didn't want you to be worried and all that.'
MOTHER: 'Well, I *am* worried.'

And so on . . . The communication is open. The mother's intuition proved correct, and hopefully now mother and daughter will be able to discuss the issues and reach some kind of compromise. Even if they don't, at least now the mother knows where her daughter is going.

There are so many voices, both external and internal, telling us what we 'should' do as a parent, that often it's hard to trust our own authority. You may have conflicting views about what you 'should' or 'shouldn't' let your teenager do, in addition to any actual conflict you might be experiencing with him or her. In fact, the more we are in conflict with ourselves, the more likely we will find ourselves battling things out with our teenager – almost as if our inner conflict becomes externalised sometimes.

If this is true for you, work at reducing your inner conflict and strengthening your inner voice. If you are constantly giving yourself a hard time – that is, criticising yourself – try to be a bit more gentle with yourself. Trust yourself. Affirm inwardly, 'I am doing the best I can,' or 'I hold myself in gentle and loving esteem.' This can help you build your inner strength and feel more calm.

Listen to your *friendly* inner voice, the one that pops up from time to time with words of encouragement and helpful suggestions. Tune in to this inner guide whenever possible – make a daily appointment, preferably, a time for quiet reflection. It's really important – especially during the trials and tribulations of the teenage years – to allow yourself to be guided by your inner wisdom. The more you are in touch with that, the more you build your inner strength. And the more you are likely to encourage your teenager to trust his or her intuition as well. This will put him or her in good stead in all kinds of situations.

Trust your feelings, as well, about your teenager. If she or he is behaving in a way that may seem odd to other people but feels all right to you, then there is probably no problem. On the other hand, if the behaviour starts *not* to feel all right, it's better to say so. 'I'm worried that you're spending so much time on the computer' may be an opening to discussion. Always check out feelings or intuition. And always 'own' what you say – in other words, say 'I' – 'I'm concerned' or 'I'm unclear' – rather than 'You worry me' or 'You make me confused'. Instead of being at the mercy of your worst imaginings, this allows you to test whether your intuition is accurate or not. Then you can coolly evaluate the situation and decide on a course of action if necessary.

Easing internal as well as external pressure can help you feel stronger and calmer when communicating with your teenager.

Chapter Three
COMMUNICATING ABOUT BEHAVIOUR

UNDERSTANDING BEHAVIOUR

Behaviour itself is a form of communication. Just as attitude communicates itself, so behaviour usually communicates something. A teenager who is driving everyone in the family mad with their loud music may be signalling some underlying feeling or need: for example, a need to rebel or to feel jubilant. All behaviour in adults and children is driven by some need – for example, the need to eat, to feel safe, the need for attention. Sometimes the need is obvious and conscious; sometimes it is hidden and unconscious. Sometimes behaviour compensates for the need: for example, someone who needs support may feel angry and hurt at not having it and so goes out and smashes something instead.

If a teenager keeps shutting herself or himself in the bedroom, she or he may have a need for privacy, or may be expressing a need to prove her or his independence. Even if your teenager is reluctant to communicate about what's going on, you may sometimes be able to pick up signals from his or her behaviour. Then, instead of asking about the behaviour, you might be able to identify the *need*. Sometimes, just accepting the need, even though there may be nothing you yourself can do about it, can make it easier to understand the behaviour. However, *accepting the need does not mean you accept the behaviour.* If the behaviour is unacceptable, you must say so.

Much of teenagers' behaviour is symptomatic of the many changes going on for them. They have many needs that may be unconscious but which can be almost overwhelming. Some examples of these needs are:

- the need for independence. It's important to encourage independence – different degrees of independence depending, of course, on the individual's level of maturity. This can be a bumpy ride, especially as sometimes *they* feel ready for certain things and *we* feel they're not!;
- the need to stay up all night sometimes – probably nature's way of helping them get in training for when they will be sexually active. It can also be the need for rebellion;
- the need to sleep (like babies and younger children, they seem to grow in their sleep);
- the need for stimulation;
- the need to feel confident;
- the need to escape from reality sometimes (behaviour such as turning to drugs is sometimes an attempt to meet these last three needs);
- the need for support;
- the need for approval;
- the need for disapproval (sometimes), and
- the need to be taken seriously.

Sometimes disruptive behaviour at school is a symptom of educational needs not being met. An adolescent may be struggling with some school subjects or feeling frustrated and not be receiving adequate support. Educational needs are extremely important. Helping a teenager get those needs met is always an investment in her or his wellbeing.

If we understand what they are communicating through their behaviour, we can help teenagers understand and recognise their own needs.

We need to be able to help ourselves as well, and look after our own needs. For example, someone who gets angry easily may have an underlying unmet need. The more we take care of our own needs, the better – and the more relaxed space we will be in to communicate.

Jill regularly used to lose her rag at her son Damien, aged fourteen, especially when he arrived home from school in the evenings. This coincided with her own arrival home from work, when she was feeling exhausted. At the suggestion of her counsellor, she started taking a nap when she first arrived home. 'It works wonders,' she said. 'I'm in a better mood these days, and Damien's left in peace. He fixes himself something to eat if he's hungry, and sometimes makes a meal for me as well.'

By addressing her own needs Jill realised that it was her own behaviour and not her son's that needed adjusting. That simple adjustment helped improve communication between her and her son.

THE DIFFERENCE BETWEEN NEEDS AND WANTS

It's important to make a distinction between 'needing' something and 'wanting' something. All human beings have universal needs: the need to eat or sleep or feel a sense of belonging. Wants, on the other hand, are more sophisticated: for example, I may want to go to the cinema and you may want to go shopping.

If your teenage son says, 'I *need* those trainers' (which, incidentally, cost hundreds of pounds), he may be confusing 'need' with 'want'. What he is really saying is that he wants those particular trainers. The underlying *need*, however, may be for a new pair of shoes, which you may or may not be able to help him with. The need may also be to gain acceptance or approval from the peer group. It may be possible to meet this in another way, such as still observing the 'dress code' but in an original and individual manner.

Helping your son or daughter become clear about the difference between something she or he wants and needs may help him or her meet real needs rather than chase unrealistic wants, which sometimes hide real needs. It may also help him or her withstand some of the fiercer pressures of commercialism – as well as saving yourself quite a bit of money.

GIVING AN ASSERTIVE MESSAGE

If you find your teenager's behaviour difficult, you will probably make things easier by asking him or her to change his or her *behaviour* rather than requiring him or her to change as a person. Yet it's surprising how often we attack the person rather than criticise the behaviour. For example, instead of yelling 'You stupid, selfish idiot, playing that racket so loud', which will lead only to more yelling and shouting from your teenager, try stating calmly what the behaviour is and the effect it's having on you. For example, 'When you play your music so loud, I feel annoyed because I can't concentrate on what I'm doing.'

This has all the components of an assertive message. These are:

1. State what the behaviour is ('When you do such-and-such').
2. Say how you feel ('I feel annoyed/sad/irritated').
3. State the effect ('I can't get on with my work').

It's important to state what you want to happen as well:

PARENT: 'What I want you to do is turn it down.'
TEENAGER: 'But it *has* to be this loud.'

At least there's talking. You may then have to negotiate the terms: for example, agree that it is acceptable to have the music loud at a different time of day, or compromise on what is an acceptable level now. This way you are more likely to succeed in asking your teenager to change his or her behaviour without the whole scene escalating into a full-scale row.

THE EFFECTS OF NEGATIVE ATTENTION

Often, giving negative attention to unacceptable behaviour can reinforce that behaviour, especially if the behaviour is done out of a need for attention in the first place. It's a well-known fact that even young children prefer 'negative strokes' – such as being shouted at – to no strokes at all: that is, negative attention is preferable to no attention. This may be a pattern that has built up with your child, and now that he or she is a teenager the behaviour and needs have grown more extreme. In these cases it is worth practising giving attention only to acceptable behaviour – that is, giving *positive* attention and ignoring other behaviours.

It is amazing sometimes how, when particular behaviour in a teenager is no longer an issue for a parent, the behaviour can quietly fade away. Giving negative attention can be like a game of cat and mouse between parent and child: when the cat stops chasing, the mouse stops running because there's no point in playing the game. Behaviour itself is neutral. Even though you still hear parents exhorting their children to 'behave', we are all 'behaving' in one form or another all the time. Even when we're asleep we are behaving, in that we are sleeping. When we're speaking, we're behaving in that we are speaking. Behaviour is either acceptable or unacceptable, depending on who is doing *what, where, how* and *with whom*.

What's acceptable to me might not be acceptable to you, and vice versa. This can also be true of two parents in the same family. Negotiation then has to take place between parents, and possibly other family members, as well as between parents and teenagers, in which all parties are able to state their needs. (That's when the real fun begins.) Although much is said about the need for parents to be consistent, there are times when it is not possible for two parents to put on a 'united front'. This can be a useful life lesson for your teenager – that is, to recognise that every individual, *including parents*, is a person in his or her own right, with his or her own opinions and needs.

BEHAVIOUR THAT AFFECTS OTHERS

Attempting to get your teenager to change a particular way of behaving just because you think they 'shouldn't' be behaving in that way can be a waste of precious energy. For effective results, concentrate on behaviour that impinges on your, or others' *personal space*. For example, if your teenager's room is in a mess, but you don't actually *have* to look at it, save your breath. It is actually not your problem. Your teenager, presumably, is responsible for his or her own room. (If not, then you *may* have a problem.) If, however, the mess from the room is beginning to spread into other areas that affect you, you probably need to say something.

When you communicate about it, you can make it clear that such behaviour is unacceptable, rather than go on about 'bad' behaviour. For example, 'I don't mind your room being a mess – that's up to you – but I do mind having clothes all over the floor of the hall and bathroom.'

This is better, and more effective, than saying, 'Such untidy behaviour is *disgraceful*,' or words to that effect. Use the assertive 'formula' if necessary:

'When you leave your clothes lying around I get

cross because it means I end up being the one to pick them up.'

Remember to say 'I' – for example, 'I find this behaviour unacceptable' – which is personally 'owning' what you feel, rather than say 'You're no good' or 'It's unacceptable'.

Remember to state what you want to happen as well: 'What I'd like you to do is clear up your clothes from the hall and confine your mess to your own area.'

This makes it easier for your teenager to change his or her behaviour. Or, put another way, it makes it harder for him or her to argue with you.

It also makes it possible for him or her to say: 'Well, what *I* would like is for you to get off my back, OK?'

Which is fine: it's an assertive statement in return and – as long as she or he picks up the fifteen T-shirts from the hall – helps him or her do what's required as well as keeping his or her dignity.

APPROACHING PROBLEMS

It helps to detach a problem from the person or persons concerned. For example, if your daughter hasn't washed for a week, she may well smell. Is this a problem for her? Maybe not. For you (and presumably anyone else) it's a problem if you come into close contact with her. But your *daughter* is not the problem, only her odour. You may well say you don't want her joining you at mealtimes, and she may agree to take her meals in her room. End of problem. If you continue to make your *daughter* the problem, conflict is almost bound to follow.

If something bothers you about your teenager's behaviour, it may be a problem only for you and not a problem for him or her. And vice versa: *you* might enjoy doing something – for example, dancing naked to candlelight every evening – which presents a problem for your teenager. If you can identify *what* and *whose* the problem is, you will find it easier to communicate rather than get into a big conflict about it.

Returning to the classic situation of the hopelessly untidy bedroom (the teenager's, that is, not yours), ask yourself, 'Where does this problem belong?' If the teenager doesn't seem concerned about the mess, then it is definitely *not* his or her problem. If, however, the mess is driving you mad, then this is *your* problem, and you need to address it as such. If you're communicating about it, say, 'I have a problem with your room being so untidy,' rather than, 'You're a disgrace, and if you don't tidy your room in the next twenty-four hours you're getting no pocket money.'

You may find that you're a parent who is worried that your teenager's room is *too tidy*. Again, ask yourself, 'Is this my problem or his problem?' You may be worrying that this is not 'normal' behaviour for a teenager, and that therefore the problem is his. But, again, if it doesn't seem to be a problem for him, it may just be your problem. If so, ask yourself, 'Is this *really* a problem?' You may only be making it one because you think it *should* be. Be guided by your intuition in these matters. Even if your teenager's behaviour seems odd – for example, if she or he spends time each day singing to crystals or talking to a hat – if it's not a problem for her or him *or* for you, then there is probably nothing to worry about. The important thing is to keep an eye on things, so that you are aware if the behaviour is becoming over-obsessive or addictive or taking the teenager over in some way.

If you are worried, express your concern – without making a drama. It might be worth having a quiet word with a teacher to check if your teenager is displaying any signs of abnormal behaviour at school. If not, the behaviour is evidently not adversely affecting his or her life. If, on the other hand, you are worried that the behaviour *is* seriously off-balance, you would be wise to seek the advice of your family doctor.

DIFFERENT STYLES OF COMMUNICATION

In communicating about behaviour, our level of success depends greatly on our style of communication. Communication styles fall broadly into the following categories:

- passive;
- aggressive;
- manipulative (sometimes described as 'passive aggressive'), and
- assertive.

If you have a *passive* style, you probably have a fairly permissive or *laissez-faire* approach to your teenager – possibly to the point of being a 'doormat' and letting her or him walk all over you. This can lead to rebellion, where the teenager feels a need to keep pushing and pushing until she or he feels a boundary.

If, on the other hand, you have a fairly *aggressive*

style of communicating, you probably have a tendency to be assertive, and possibly violent towards your teenager – verging on a bullying style of parenting. This, too, may breed rebellion. Both styles can lead to a lack of confidence in a teenager, by making him or her feel neglected or attacked.

These are examples from two opposite ends of the spectrum, and most of us lie somewhere in between. (In fact, the majority of parents seem to have amazing powers of tolerance and then – boom! – they lose their temper as a bull at a red rag.)

Manipulative behaviour is a form of 'passive aggression' – indirect, sneaky aggression. This can mean withdrawal, or a refusal to cooperate, or the underhand sabotage of arrangements. It can also take the form of emotional blackmail.

Best of all is *assertive* communication, where parents *and* teenagers can state their needs. In the game of communication, the stakes are as follows:

> Aggressive communication: I WIN, YOU LOSE;
> Manipulative communication: I WIN, YOU LOSE;
> Passive communication: YOU WIN, I LOSE, and
> Assertive communication: I WIN, YOU WIN.

Assertive communication is based on:

- respect;
- equality of needs;
- the knowledge that each person has rights, and
- valuing the other person and oneself.

It requires practice and sometimes effort – especially when negotiating needs – but generally makes for more effective and rewarding communication for both parents and teenagers.

COMMUNICATION AS A TWO-WAY PROCESS

To communicate effectively, parents and teenagers need to be able to listen to one another and engage in dialogue. Two-way communication is talking *and* listening.

We've seen how extremely passive or aggressive styles of communication can lead to trouble. In both cases, the communication is one-way: in the case of aggression, the parent 'attacks' the teenager (verbally or otherwise); in the case of very passive behaviour, the parent may be neglectful, or in a state of *non*-communication with the teenager, in which case it is possibly the teenager's communication that is one-way.

'She/he doesn't listen to me any more' is a constant lament I hear from parents of teenagers. But the question is: does the parent listen to the teenager? And, if so, what is the quality of the listening?

When parents tell me they have this problem, we sit down together and discuss:

1) the teenager's behaviour, and
2) the parents' style of communication.

One of the questions we consider is: is the style of communication appropriate to the situation? For example, if a parent rants and raves at a teenager for not doing the washing-up, is such an approach really going to change things? It will probably make the teenager even more reluctant to do that and other chores. If, on the other hand, the teenager arrived home very late at night and the parents were worried about him or her, such a reaction would be more appropriate (though not necessarily more effective). Or, in a situation where a teenager arrived home very late and the parents *ignored* her or him, this could leave a void of unspoken communication. To enable two-way communication, a rewrite of the script might go something like this:

SCENE ONE – THE KITCHEN SINK

FATHER: 'I'm really angry that you haven't done the washing-up.'

DAUGHTER (*sniggering*): 'Sorry, Dad, I never got round to it. I had to go out, see, and then when I got back I had my homework to do, didn't I?'

FATHER: 'Yes, but you said you'd do it, remember?'

DAUGHTER: 'Oh God, here we go again. Can't you just leave me alone?'

FATHER (*calmly, hanging on in there*): 'When I make a commitment to do something I try to keep it, and I'd like you to do the same.'

DAUGHTER: 'I know, but I just haven't had *time*, Dad. Anyway, washing-up isn't just women's work.'

FATHER: 'I agree. It was my turn yesterday, and it will be my turn again tomorrow. I know you haven't had much time. Will you do it now, please?'

DAUGHTER (*grumble, grumble*): 'Oh all right, then.' (*More grumbles. Proceeds to do washing-up loudly.*)

Two-way communication: the father clearly stated his feelings *and* listened to his daughter. He said 'I' ('I'm really angry' and 'When I make a commitment to do something') rather than 'you' (he could have said 'You never do the washing-up'), which helped to keep communication open and focused on the job in hand instead of putting all the attention on the teenager. His attitude helped as well: staying calm while still being able to express what he felt about the situation.

SCENE TWO – THE LIVING-ROOM, THREE A.M.

Two parents anxiously await the return of their son. Son arrives; lurches in through the front door.

PARENT 1: 'What time do you call this?'

PARENT 2: 'Where do you think you've been?'

SON: 'Yeah, well . . . ' (*makes to exit towards his bedroom*)

PARENT 1: 'We need to talk. Please come back and sit down.' (*son cusses under breath and flops into armchair*)

PARENT 2: 'We've been really worried about you. You said you'd be back by midnight.'

SON: 'Well, it wasn't my fault.'

PARENT 1: 'What happened, then?'

SON: 'I missed the last bus, then Jason said he'd give me a lift but he'd had too much to drink so we decided to leave the car and walk.'

Parents breathe a double sigh of relief: not only had their son returned in one piece, he and Jason had made a sensible decision as well.

Two-way communication: the parents, although understandably upset and anxious, stated their need to talk, thus avoiding a confrontation. They also stated their feelings in a way that helped to keep communication open – 'We've been really worried', rather than 'You made us worried' or 'How could you do this to us?'. The conversation will also pave the way to negotiating coming-home times in future.

SCENE THREE – A DIFFERENT LIVING-ROOM, TEN P.M.

Daughter arrives looking dishevelled.

DAUGHTER: 'Hi, Mum, I'm back.'

MOTHER: 'Hi.'

DAUGHTER: 'Anything good on telly?'

MOTHER: 'Some old film.'

DAUGHTER: 'Well, I won't bother then. I'm sick to
   death of the same old crap.' (*throws her bag across
   the room and exits towards bedroom*)

MOTHER: 'Hey! Come back and talk!'

DAUGHTER: 'Why should I? You never talk to me.
   You're never interested in anything I do.'

MOTHER: 'I *am* interested. I just don't always show it.
   When you were angry about the TV programmes
   just now, I thought you might be angry with me.'

(*Daughter flops down on a chair.*)

DAUGHTER (*in disbelief and amazement*): 'Let's talk, then.'

Two-way communication: after a habitual pattern of ignoring her daughter, this parent read the signs (that her daughter was angry) and *stated* what she saw. She broke a pattern and took the risk of *inviting* communication. Both mother and daughter started to talk about issues they had been avoiding. It's just a beginning, and arguments may follow. But even arguing is two-way communication and helps to keep communication alive.

THE STRUGGLE FOR CONTROL

As teenagers move towards independence, parents find it increasingly hard to 'control' their teenagers' behaviour. The trouble is, the attempt to *control* behaviour is what can cause problems. Teenagers are at a stage of development in life where they need their parents to let go of control rather than hold on.

If parents try to hold on too tightly to control, this can lead to rebellious behaviour in teenagers. Or, a teenager may develop extremes of behaviour in an attempt to take control herself or himself. For example, she or he may do something that is guaranteed to wind up her or his parents, such as refusing to eat or going in for multiple body-piercing. The more attention the parents give to such behaviour, the more the teenager is in control.

Beware of the dynamic of control: you may find yourself unwittingly drawn into a conflict about behaviour which has nothing to do with behaviour at all.

CONSEQUENCES

Part of enabling your teenager to grow into a respon-sible adult is letting her or him discover the consequences of her or his behaviour. Letting go of control doesn't mean giving your teenager free rein to do whatever she or he likes. It is more about gradually allowing her or him to take responsibility for her or his life. Note the word *gradually*: for example, agreeing that she or he can stay out late one night a week for starters. Or, if he develops obnoxious habits, such as not washing, let him take responsibility for that and understand the consequences: it's his choice, and the consequence is that you do not want him joining you at mealtimes. Make it clear that this is not a punishment but a result of behaviour that you find unpleasant. (He may in fact find that friends in his peer group have a similar if not stronger response.)

By allowing teenagers to make their own decisions, we help them learn about the consequences of their decisions. If we don't allow them to do so, we hinder their chances of learning to be responsible. Consequences can be short term and long term. For example, not doing revision for exams might give more freedom in the short term but could affect education and job prospects in the long term.

Chapter Four
SETTING BOUNDARIES

THE VALUE OF BOUNDARIES

Teenagers, like children of any age, need boundaries. And boundaries change as children and teenagers grow older. Just as a toddler needs a safety gate at the top of the stairs, a teenager needs clear demarcations as to where and how far she or he can go. As well as applying to space, boundaries can apply to time – for example, an agreed time to be home by is a boundary – and behaviour – for example, defining what is acceptable or unacceptable behaviour. Boundaries are necessary because:

- they provide an appropriate degree of safety;
- they provide security, by letting a teenager know where she or he stands;
- they help a teenager feel cared for and valued;
- they give a basis from which to explore and make it safe to go to the edge;
- they provide clear guidelines for a teenager to follow;
- they can be put to the test: pushing against a boundary helps a teenager ascertain whether or not it is real;

- they provide something for a teenager to kick against in order to grow. It is only natural that, when a child can run up or down stairs, she or he doesn't need a safety gate any more. In the same way, a young teenager who had to be home by nine in the evening will kick against (or climb over) the same boundary (if it's still there) when she or he is older;
- they help teenagers look after themselves, and others, by learning to set limits on their own behaviour;
- they provide an opportunity to negotiate (sometimes), and
- they provide opportunities for teenagers to set their own boundaries. These are often the most effective boundaries of all. For example, if a parent says to a teenager, 'Here's a tenner for the school trip – I want some change back,' and the teenager protests, saying, 'No, that's not enough,' it may not be worth continuing along the lines of 'If you don't give me any change there'll be trouble . . . ' because the teenager will probably ignore the boundary and spend the money anyway. It is more effective to say, 'Well, how much money do you think you need?' The teenager will then probably attempt to stretch the boundary and say something like 'thirty pounds'. Both parties having stated their position, now is the time to negotiate:

PARENT: 'OK, so you'd like thirty pounds. What do you think is a *reasonable* amount?'

TEENAGER: 'Fifteen pounds? I could probably manage

on ten, but we've got to buy lunch and drinks and I'd like to buy some souvenirs as well.'

PARENT: 'So you think you could manage on ten?'

TEENAGER: 'Mmm. But I'd like a bit more, just in case. Could you manage fifteen? If I don't spend it all I'll give you back the change.'

PARENT: 'All right, then.' (*mutters under breath about the cost of living*)

Setting boundaries is a significant part of the parenting role, and children and teenagers usually *expect* to have boundaries. Sometimes a teenager feels a sense of relief when a boundary is set, even though outwardly he or she may grumble about it. Without boundaries, a child or teenager may feel very insecure. She or he may develop extremes of behaviour in order to test boundaries that aren't really there. If boundaries are too rigid, on the other hand, she or he may feel oppressed and compelled to pit herself or himself against them.

The most important thing to remember is that, with teenagers, boundaries are not made of steel; they are flexible and open to negotiation. Boundaries that help a child or teenager to feel supported are more effective than a heavy hand.

COOPERATION V. CONTROL

Once children become teenagers, boundaries are more about cooperation and negotiation than control. Because of the imbalance in power between an adult and child, it is easier (though not necessarily healthy) for parents to control young children. However, with teenagers it's more difficult. Your role as a parent is much more to guide and contain than 'control'. Just as the banks of a river help to hold and control the flow of the water, the role of a parent is to help to hold and control the *flow* of the teenager and, like water, the teenager has a life of his or her own. The most successful parent-teenager relationship is the one where parents and teenager *work together* to help the flow. Gradually giving more responsibility to your teenager is a cooperative and organic process.

Attempting to impose too much control on your teenager can be a way of asking for trouble, leading to anger and rebellion in the young person, or – if she or he *submits* to such control – to opting out of responsibility. (Letting the parents do all the work can be a convenient way of avoiding growing up.) It can also lead to low self-esteem and lack of confidence, which may be carried into adulthood. Teenagers who have not been set adequate boundaries, on the other hand, may have a tendency to take over control or go out of control themselves.

Often, when a teenager oversteps boundaries, parents tend to punish him or her or impose sanctions – by grounding him or her, for example. This may be effective, and necessary, *on occasions*, but if it is too much of a regular occurrence, it may serve only to perpetuate the teenager's behaviour. Parents, and teenager, become trapped in a cycle of control-punishment, control-punishment which can be hard to break.

A way of changing this may be to take a problem-solving approach to a particular situation rather than automatically imposing control. Parents should see it as a *shared* problem and talk about it with their teenager, asking 'How are we going to sort this out?' (rather than 'What are you going to do about it?'). This opens the possibility of discussion and negotiation, and helps the teenager learn to take responsibility.

HOLDING FIRM

If, as a parent, you are struggling to set boundaries for your teenager and wondering 'Where have I gone wrong?', you would do better to reassess your position than blame yourself for failing to be effective. Like the riverbank, you can only do what you're there to do – sometimes you feel swamped and sometimes the river floods its banks. And even if you or your teenager have 'messed up', or you have failed sometimes in your attempt to set boundaries, see it all as being part of a process that is still going on. Boundaries sometimes slip, or may no longer be appropriate.

Here are some suggestions for setting adequate boundaries:

- *Be clear where the boundary is.* For example, there is no point in saying 'Be back on time' if it is not clear *what* time, or in criticising behaviour if you don't say what is acceptable or unacceptable behaviour.
- *Hold your ground.* Having set a limit, you may well be challenged by your teenager, so it's important to know what your bottom line is and to stick to it. Keep repeating your message, if necessary. For example, 'You can't stay out late on Monday

nights.' It helps to use the 'stuck record' technique (for those of us who remember gramophones), to keep calmly saying the same thing over and over.

- *Field the response.* If your teenager kicks up a fuss, calmly *listen* to what she or he has to say, which includes allowing her or him to make her or his feelings known and state what she or he would like to happen. She or he might make a verbally abusive response, in which case remain calm until she or he has finished. Then calmly refute any criticism – for example, 'No, I am not a sad case,' and repeat the request: 'No, I am not a sad case, and the bottom line is that I don't want you staying out late on Monday nights.'

- *Avoid being diverted by other issues.* Your teenager may try to wriggle out of the subject or throw in additional complications. Stay focused on the issue in question.

- *Be willing to shift a little.* Be prepared to negotiate if possible. Negotiating a solution to a problem may mean having to change your position slightly.

THE ART OF NEGOTIATION

Much of the art of negotiation is being able to hold your ground *and* shift your position if necessary. The more you practise, the more your teenager will become adept at it as well. You could even get to enjoy the process. Negotiation can be nerve-racking; it can also be extremely satisfying when both parties arrive at an acceptable solution. Negotiation is about *sharing responsibility* with your teenager and treating her or him on a more equal basis. This in itself can help her or him be more responsible.

Here are some negotiating tools:

- *Clearly state your position.* PARENT: 'I want you home by eleven o'clock.'
- *Listen calmly to the response.* TEENAGER: 'You never let me stay out late. All my friends are allowed to.' Etc., etc.
- *Identify the teenager's position.* PARENT: 'What time would you *like* to come home?' TEENAGER: 'Three a.m.'
- *State whether this is acceptable or unacceptable.* PARENT: 'I'm sorry, that's totally unacceptable.'
- *Invite alternatives.* Continue to listen to your teenager's response, and ask if he or she has any other suggestions. The teenager might suggest a slightly more reasonable time, or that she or he stays the night with a friend.
- *Know your bottom line.* While you might be willing to shift your position on the actual time – say, for example, you shift from your original time of eleven o'clock and agree to midnight – you need to know at what point you are going to stand firm. Your bottom line might be 'Midnight, and not a minute later', or 'You stay at your friend's house rather than travel home on your own.'
- *Listen to needs.* Allow your teenager to state her or his needs: 'I need to stay to the end of the disco.' This can be the tricky part: being able to hold your ground *and* listen. Listen, and state your own needs as well: 'I need to know you're safe.'
- *Do a deal.* 'All right, I will provide transport. I'll

pick you up at midnight, so long as you agree to
do the shopping this afternoon.'

What started off as a dispute over time turned into a
recognition of needs. Both parent and teenager
successfully negotiated their way to a solution. The
parent, especially, mastered the art of being able to
hold her ground *and* listen to her teenager. This is the
knack of being able to go in and out of 'neutral' before
re-engaging gear.

SAYING NO

Sometimes there is no room for negotiation, as in the
following example:

CHERYL: *I was with Wayne and his friend, and Wayne kept
asking if his friend could stay over. I said no. He'd had
friends to stay the last few weekends, and this weekend I
needed some space. Wayne still kept on asking me, in front
of his friend, trying to get me to compromise and asking if
the friend could just stay Friday night and not Saturday
night. In the end I blew my top. I said 'No, I'm not having
it. No means NO.' I was very angry and he was upset, but
that was my bottom line. He ran off for a couple of hours and
I had a good cry, I was so choked and angry. But next day
we were able to talk about it.*

One of the most effective ways of setting a limit is to
say 'no'. Just saying 'no' is not always easy for the
parent of a teenager. However, 'no' is a powerful word,
and there are many ways of saying it. It can be shouted,

yelled, muttered or whispered. What matters is that when you say 'no' you mean 'no'.

What matters even more is that your teenager learns from your example how to say 'no'. Saying 'no' is an important life skill for any teenage boy or girl to have, and one that will help him or her set *personal* boundaries in many situations.

'No' itself is a boundary which is sometimes easy to shift. Most of us can be persuaded, at some time or another, to change our 'no' into 'yes'. However, when there is an absolute 'no' by a parent, a teenager knows when to stop – that is, when the parent is absolutely resolute and clear, and the bottom line has been drawn. Depending on your teenager's response, you may have to use all your willpower to hold your ground. Remember the 'stuck record' technique, and avoid giving lengthy explanations as to why you are saying 'no'. Keep things short and to the point: 'No, I can't let you have money for clothes this week.'

If your teenager has strong feelings, acknowledge those feelings and repeat your message. For example, 'I know you're upset, but I'm sorry, I don't have money for clothes this week.'

If you seem to have reached an impasse, don't give in. Instead, say, 'We seem to have reached a deadlock. What shall we do?' This opens the door for discussion. By holding your 'no' position, you and your teenager can now move into the next stage of communication.

Remember, saying 'yes' wholeheartedly is possible only if we know how to say 'no'. Without 'no', 'yes' has little meaning.

STATING YOUR PERSONAL BOUNDARIES

There is usually a reason for setting boundaries. Either it is for the wellbeing of your teenager or of other people, or it's to take care of your own needs. For example, 'It's one o'clock in the morning and I need to get some sleep. Will you turn the music off now, please.' The setting of this personal need is more likely to enlist cooperation, or at least negotiation, than if you communicate it as a general, impartial boundary, such as 'Turn the music off; it's one o'clock.' If your teenager understands the need for the boundary she or he is more likely to cooperate, or if she or he has agreed to it previously as a ground rule.

It's important to 'own' your needs. 'I need sleep/I need peace/I need to know you're safe.' This can take the onus off the teenager and give her or him the opportunity to choose to respect your needs. (This is different from emotional blackmail, where you make the other person responsible for your needs – for example, 'How could you *do this* to me?')

Sometimes this process is helped by stating your feelings. 'I'm anxious that you might get into trouble' has a very different feel from, 'Watch out – you're always getting into trouble.'

Setting our own personal boundaries helps our teenagers learn about setting theirs.

SEEKING REINFORCEMENT

At times the river may burst its banks and reinforcements are necessary. The reinforcement of boundaries can take the form of the army in the case of the river or, in the case of a teenager, the police, counsellors and/ or the local authorities. It can be distressing, and sometimes terrifying to see a teenager go out of control, or become psychologically disturbed or involved in criminal activities. In these kinds of situations, it's important to recognise our own limitations, and we may have to stand back and let the professionals take over.

However much you've tried to relinquish control and give your teenager responsibility, she or he may be at a stage in life where she or he is unable to take it. She or he may resort to extremes of behaviour which provoke you, and others, to take back control. In these cases the teenager probably has a *strong need* to be controlled at this point in time and may need firmer controls than you are able to give.

Some situations are too dangerous or too difficult for you to handle on your own. If your teenager is in trouble with the law, or involved with probation or psychiatric services, for example, you would be advised to take full advantage of the help that is on offer. These agencies may be able to help set appropriate boundaries for your son or daughter. At the same time, you may need to seek legal or independent medical advice to represent the short- and long-term interests of your son or daughter.

This can be an extremely trying time for a parent, but it is important to conserve your energy and keep as accepting and supportive an attitude as possible. The best way to do so is to seek support for yourself as well. (See 'Useful Addresses', page 141.)

For lesser transgressions of boundaries, it may still be necessary to take drastic measures. Sometimes the act of grounding a teenager – keeping her or him in for a certain period of time as a result of misdemeanours – can be effective in reinforcing limits. Sometimes a teenager may even welcome such a measure (even though outwardly, of course, she or he may grumble) because:

- it is an acknowledgement of guilt (that boundaries have been broken);
- it is a means of providing safety and security: a teenager may be relieved to have enforced time at home for a while if things have been getting a bit risky or out of control in her or his life, and
- it provides street cred: 'I can't come out. I'm grounded.'

However, my advice would be to use this measure sparingly. If it happens too often it may not be taken seriously. Furthermore, it is a kind of punishment, and punishment is not necessarily the best way of changing behaviour or helping a teenager take control of his or her own life. *Trust* in his or her abilities and, however scary this may be, knowing all the risks involved, remind yourself that *you* survived those teenage years.

Chapter Five
COMMUNICATION BREAKDOWN OR BREAKTHROUGH?

As a teenager grows more independent of his or her parents, the transition of breaking away can be a gradual one or it can be a series of traumatic shudders and bumps. Communication can veer from full-on confrontation to total withdrawal.

THE NEED NOT TO COMMUNICATE

Sometimes it can be hard to accept our teenagers' independence, especially in early adolescence, when we may still look on them as children. I often hear parents say in despair, 'She's always sulking,' or 'He locks himself in his room all day.' Whether your teenager withdraws physically or emotionally, this is more than likely part of the separation process. It may be painful for you, the parent, because it seems as if you can't get through which, in fact, is the whole point: for the young person to demonstrate independence and put up a barrier between herself or himself and you.

Often a teenager whose room is in a total mess is

doing just this: she or he is asserting independence and taking control of her or his territory.

PARENTS KEEP OUT

An adolescent who, as a child, never shut the door may now ask to have a lock fitted on his or her bedroom door. Respecting this kind of wish is wiser than making a big deal about it, for example by saying, 'We never have locked doors in *this* house.' Teenagers can also be extremely self-conscious about their changing bodies and have a greater need for privacy than before. If you accept your teenager's withdrawal into his or her own little world as a natural part of growing up, you will make it easier for him or her to re-emerge eventually (which they usually do, with a vengeance!). If, on the other hand, you are intolerant and make it difficult for them, you could push them even further into withdrawal.

Incidentally, it is still possible to communicate even when they are in withdrawal. Sometimes they appreciate a bit of contact or interest or to hear the sound of your voice or have the occasional (friendly) note pushed under the door. (It could even be an opportunity for you to practise Morse code.) If your son or daughter seems to be addicted to computer games or spends all weekend on a computer, encourage him or her to take regular breaks (for health reasons, both mental and physical), or if your teenager spends all his or her time watching TV in his or her room, he or she could feel isolated if that is the only option. If you want to see your teenager sometimes, it's worth making sure there are times when the whole family is together.

If you are worried that your teenager is depressed, it is advisable to go with him or her to see your family doctor, who may refer him or her to a counsellor or child guidance officer. There are also a number of helplines available for teenagers to talk about anything that might be troubling them. There are helplines for parents as well. (See 'Useful Addresses', page 141.)

DIFFERENT KINDS OF CONFLICT

Conflict is almost inevitable in the changing relationship between parent and teenager. There are many kinds of conflict, from a minor row between parent and teenager to a full-scale family drama. Many different kinds of *situations* can also cause conflict. For example:

- You disapprove of your son's or daughter's behaviour, such as smoking or drinking alcohol.
- You and your teenager disagree about what time he or she should return home at night.
- Your teenager refuses to do any chores/do any homework, or may refuse to go to school.
- You and your teenager have an argument about money.
- You disapprove of your teenager's girlfriend/boyfriend.

Most of us know that each of these situations can be highly charged with emotion. For example, disapproving of your teenager's girlfriend or boyfriend could be a minor irritation or it could be a desperate Romeo and Juliet scenario. The fact is, she or he is probably going to go out with him or her anyway, and there's very little you can do to stop them. It's probably better to accept and come to terms with the relationship and hope that it doesn't last. If, however, you suspect that drugs or bullying or violence are involved, you have a legal duty to protect your son or daughter. You could ask for help from the police or a social worker, or by ringing a helpline. (See 'Useful Addresses', page 141.)

A lot depends on how you, as the parent, handle the conflict, in whatever situation. It helps to know what kind of conflict you're dealing with:

DIFFERENT NEEDS

Some conflicts arise because different individuals have different needs. For example, your teenager might need to stay out late socialising and you need to know she or he is safe. Or you might need to have an early night and your teenager has some friends round. Or your teenager may need an early night and *you* have some friends round. Or you and your teenager and other members of the family may all need to use the bathroom at the same time. And so on. (It happens every day, in most households, in one form or another.)

How to communicate about conflict:

1. Acknowledge: 'We have a problem here.'
2. State needs: for example, 'You need to go out and enjoy yourself, and I need to know you're safe,' or

'I need to have an early night, and you need to entertain your friends.' Be as clear and specific as possible.

3. Ask: 'How can we best sort this out?'

4. Negotiate respectfully, remembering that all needs are equal. However, some needs might be more pressing than others and it's important to identify these. For example, 'I have a job interview in the morning so I need you and your friends to keep your noise and your music low so that I can have an early night. Another night you can play it louder.'

5. Agree on a workable compromise if necessary.

DIFFERENT VALUES

Often quite serious conflict between parents and teenagers arises from a difference of opinions and values. A teenager may feel compelled to rebel against her or his parents' values, the values she or he has been brought up with. This can cause great heartache for a parent. But it is part of growing up: a teenager no longer taking parents' beliefs at face value but challenging and questioning them. This is part of the process of forming values of his or her own. For example, the son of a vegetarian family may experiment with eating meat. Or the daughter of a family whose religion prevents them from drinking alcohol may take to drinking alcohol. Or a teenager may refuse to go to bed at a particular time, or demand to know why she or he *shouldn't* be allowed to go to a festival during exams, or insist on painting her or his room in garish colours.

As a parent, ask yourself which values matter most

to you. Some values – for example, religious or spiritual values – may be embedded at the core of your being, whereas others – for example, washing up after every meal – may be negotiable with your teenager. It's important to state your values whether or not your teenager agrees with them. For example, 'To me, education is one of the most important things in life. It hurts me deeply to see you throwing your education away.'

To which the teenager might reply: 'Education matters to me too. It's just that school *sucks*. I get a better education in the pub/on the street corner/watching TV.'

Discussion of values with your teenager can help to give new perspectives on a situation of conflict. It can also help to prevent conflict sometimes, as well as giving your teenager – and you – the chance to *explore* values. What is important is to 'own' your values rather than state them as absolute fact. For example, say, 'I believe that fish shouldn't be eaten on Friday – it's part of my religion,' rather than 'It's wrong to eat fish on Friday.' Or 'I don't want people smoking in my home,' rather than 'People who smoke are antisocial.' This then gives your teenager the opportunity to talk about his or her values in the same way.

Take advantage of this opportunity to reassess and define your values. Often we hold values without even thinking about them. But imposing our values on our teenagers without any room for discussion can lead to communication breakdown.

What can be especially hard is if your teenager is growing up in a society or culture which has very different values from the country or culture you grew up in. Your teenager may conform to all kinds of dress code, social habits and beliefs which are unacceptable to you and which you possibly find offensive as well. Although this can be deeply distressing, again it helps if you are able to discuss your values with your teenager, giving your own cultural perspective and listening to your teenager as well. You may find you still share some common values.

And remember, your teenager is still in developmental mode. As a mature, independent adult, she or he may return to share some of your values. Then, again, she or he may not.

COMMUNICATING THROUGH QUARRELS

Sometimes the struggle for power, together with all the other difficult issues that parents and teenagers are dealing with, can turn a previously peaceful home into a battleground. But certain tactics will enable you to communicate your way through the battle and arrive not at victory but at peaceful solutions. You may find some of the following ideas useful in dealing with, and sometimes even preventing quarrels.

- *Deal with feelings first.* If you and your teenager are full of strong emotion, you may have to cool off and let emotions simmer down before attempting to sort out any issues. When we reach the stage of being overwhelmed by feelings, we go into 'right brain' mode – which controls feelings – and lose some of our 'left brain' capacity, which holds more rational thought. For example, if someone stamps on your foot, you might feel too hurt or too angry to engage in civilised conversation with him or her. Approaching problems rationally when we are emotionally overwhelmed is difficult. So it helps to deal with the feelings first.

For example, if you and your teenager are hurling insults at each other, try stopping one in midair and saying instead, 'I'm feeling really angry right now.'

Your teenager may then shout in reply, 'And I'm really fed up with you always telling me what to do.'

PARENT (*acknowledging feelings*): 'So I'm angry and you're fed up.'
TEENAGER: 'Yes!'

This parent, by acknowledging his own feelings, has enabled his daughter to say what she was feeling as well. The parent then let the daughter know he'd *heard* what she was feeling. This gave them both breathing space to *feel* what they were feeling, as well as some respite from verbally attacking each other.

They might now have to agree to talk about things after a cooling-off period. However, sometimes just this 'airing' of emotions in itself can help feelings to simmer down again, thus clearing the way for addressing whatever problem needs to be addressed. For example:

PARENT: 'So if you don't want me to *tell* you not to drink alcohol, how do I know you won't drink too much?'
TEENAGER: 'By trusting me.'

PARENT: 'How can I trust you when you got drunk last night?'

TEENAGER: 'Well, if you let me decide for myself and set my own limit, it would be easier for me to keep my word.'

And so on, probably leading to a discussion about what is a sensible amount to drink.

- *Feed back what you have heard.* Although in a situation of conflict you obviously have your own agenda, you will do yourself and your teenager a favour by pausing during an argument and letting her or him know what you have heard them say.

   For example, 'I hear that you resent not being told about our trip to Blackpool next weekend.'

   This helps the teenager feel heard and may stop him or her from screaming accusations at his or her parents.

PARENT CONTINUES: 'I hear that you had made other arrangements.' (*apologises if necessary*) 'We're sorry. We *could* have told you sooner, but we forgot.'

Feeding back what has been heard helps to avoid misunderstandings, especially in a quarrel where people are so full of emotion that they mishear or don't even really listen to one another. As we develop this habit, it becomes easier to ask our teenagers to feed back what they have heard us say. This helps keep channels of communication open without becoming too clogged up, therefore enabling an exploration of issues rather than a closedown:

TEENAGER: 'So you're saying I've got to come with you?'

PARENT: 'That is what we're saying, yes.'

TEENAGER: 'What if I go and stay at a friend's instead?'

PARENT: 'Is that really what you would prefer to do?'

TEENAGER: 'Yes. I'll only be miserable if I come with you.'

PARENT: 'Well . . . we'll have to think about it.'

- *State your own needs and wants.* Having fed back to your teenager what you understand his or her needs to be, briefly and clearly state your own. I say 'briefly' because being clear and succinct helps to keep to the issue in hand. Conflicts can be very messy if people's needs are spilling all over the place in an unfocused or unstated way. For example:

PARENT: 'I need to enjoy myself this weekend. I also wanted the whole family to be there.'

After discussion, this parent may decide that her need to enjoy herself is more important than her wish for all the family to be together. (Also, having a teenager who is miserable may hamper her enjoyment.)

Remember that your needs and the needs of your teenager are equally important. Conflict does not have to be a competition of needs, it is more a struggle to find a way of accommodating everyone's needs, even if it means some kind of compromise, in the end.

- *Look after your own needs.* It's important to keep your own energy level up in order to be able to do all this. It can be hard work, of marathon proportions sometimes, and requires stamina and fitness. Most important of all, you need to look after your own needs *for you.* If your needs are being met, you are more likely to feel relaxed and confident and are less likely to be drawn into battle.
- *Remember you still have power as a parent.* Whatever struggles you're engaged in, you are *still the adult in authority,* with the power to say what behaviour is acceptable or not. As long as you're still actively engaged in the parenting role, you have the right and the responsibility to lay down certain conditions. This does not mean being completely authoritarian; it means caring for yourself and caring about the welfare of your teenagers or children. It has been said that 'parenthood is not a democracy', and you have the right, sometimes, to assert this. It means being tough, if necessary, and being clear about your bottom line: for example, 'The consequences if you don't . . . are . . .' This is not necessarily a threat, because the *risks* are real. You still have a duty to protect your son or daughter if they are still legally children.
- *Know the ground rules.* It is useful if there is a set of ground rules relating to conflict in the family – for example, *no violence.* Violence tends to make matters worse in quarrels, and physically attacking

your teenager won't solve anything. With practice, some of the ideas below can help to prevent violence and lead to solutions where nobody gets hurt. In addition, the next chapter gives suggestions about the management of anger. If you're a parent with a pattern of violence towards your teenager, you may need help in changing your behaviour. (See 'Useful Addresses', page 141.)

If your teenager is violent towards you, you will have to make a plan of action for dealing with the situation if it happens again. It is better to know in advance who to call for support than to a) fight back or b) live in constant fear of it happening again. The chances are that if your teenager is violent, she or he is in need of some outside counselling or help. Violence is usually a sign of distress.

Most households have a set of ground rules operating for everyday life; often these are implicit rather than explicit. However, in the case of teenagers, especially, where so much is changing, it helps to make ground rules explicit so that both parents and teenagers know where they stand.

It may be that the ground rules that have been operating in your household for years are no longer appropriate for a growing teenager. This can be the source of many quarrels, and you and your teenager may have to sit down and renegotiate some ground rules together. For example, 'This house is a no-smoking zone' or 'No frying after nine p.m.' (You may prefer to call them 'agreements' if 'rules' sounds too much like school.) The more the teenager is involved in drawing up such agreements, the more likely she or he is to observe them. Even when she or he may break an agreement, just by reminding her or him about the agreement may help to keep her or him on track and prevent major quarrels. If quarrels occur, it may be necessary to renegotiate a particular agreement. The one thing you can be sure about with teenagers is that, as they take mighty strides towards adulthood, the goalposts do keep changing.

- *Separate your problem from theirs.* Ask yourself: '*Why* is this important to me?' or '*How* important is this to me?' Is your teenager's problem triggering something from your past, from your own experience of being a teenager? Are you over-identifying with your teenager's problem? Or are you grappling with an entirely different problem? Remember to *acknowledge to yourself* what you are feeling. You may be feeling resentful or rejected, or both. Yes, it may be that they are treating the home like a railway station and, yes, their interests *are* elsewhere. Separating your own problems from theirs might help ease the conflict.

- *'Unhook' from the drama.* It's all too easy, in quarrels, to go into *reactive* responses rather than take time to consciously respond. (This is true of all relationships, not just those with teenagers.) Dramas can be riveting, but they can be a drain on energy as well. Allowing yourself to be drawn into the drama of your teenager's life unnecessarily can be counterproductive. 'Hooking in' to drama can create more drama, with different characters playing the 'victim' or 'persecutor' or 'rescuer' role. Not that the whole of life isn't drama, but you can tone it down. 'Unhooking' is about learning the art of stepping back, disengaging: going into 'neutral' and being able to *be present and listen*, and state your position as well (listening doesn't mean you have to *agree* with what is being said), then being able to ask, 'How can you help me?' or 'How can we help each other?'

- *Brainstorm possible solutions.* Assuming you've reached the stage where you and your teenager (and possibly other members of the family as well) are talking to one another, sit down with a large sheet of paper and invite everyone to 'brainstorm' ideas of possible solutions to a problem. Write down the exact words that people say. Some of the ideas can be really outlandish. Even though they may not make perfect sense, they might contain the seed of a solution. For example, 'Send the whole family off to the moon' may mean that the family needs a holiday, and so on. Discuss the ideas once they're all down on paper, and agree on your own creative solutions.

- *Peace is not the absence of conflict.* Conflict, although painful, can be the cutting edge of learning and growth. Depending on how you handle it, communicating through conflict can provide opportunities for intimacy and new understanding between you and your teenager. Sometimes, out of the breakdown of communication comes break*through*. If you trust your abilities, and hang on in there, you may be surprisingly rewarded.

CHANGING GEAR

Sometimes you feel your home isn't your own any more. You go out for a Sunday afternoon, come home at teatime and find your main living quarters taken over by your teenager and his or her friends. Large adolescents loll around in various poses on various pieces of furniture; the TV, computer and the CD-player are on, and cups and debris are strewn over the floor. You want to scream or burst into tears, and tell them all to clear out. You just want a bit of peace and quiet, and wouldn't have minded flopping into one of those armchairs yourself. What do you do?:

- You rant and rave at your son or daughter, telling him or her to clear up the mess and insisting her or his friends leave immediately. *Congratulations!* You have acted perfectly the role of controlling parent, *and* to a full house. Result? They won't applaud, but they'll probably have a good laugh about it afterwards. The friends might even leave, but your relationship with your teenager will not be enhanced.

- You pretend everything's fine and groovy, and even whistle a tune as you hunt around the floor for a clean cup. Who are you trying to fool – yourself or them? And what's the point of trying to prove anything? Instead, notice your resentment level soaring and notice how many doors you slam.

- *You remove yourself.* (They probably haven't noticed you anyway.) This is the most effective course of action. Go immediately to your bedroom, the garden or the bathroom. Have a sob if you need to (they won't hear you) or, if you're feeling really angry, beat some cushions or scream into a cushion (if you're worried that the neighbours will hear you).

Then, having acknowledged your feelings, take a deep breath and proceed as follows:

- *Ask yourself: what do I need right now?* It may be you're hungry or desperate for a cup of tea. *See to your need first.* Be completely single-minded about it. Go back to the kitchen and brush aside any bodies and/or debris as necessary. (They probably won't notice.) Ignore any distractions, such as the state of your front room – that is not the issue just now. Stay focused on your primary objective, to make the cup of tea. Then, having made the tea:

- *Remove yourself again.* Take your tea, or your beer, or a tray of snacks to your bedroom or to the garden. Focus on whatever you're eating or drinking with absolute concentration and savour every mouthful. And relish being in the garden or your bedroom because, after all, you may be spending quite a bit of time there from now on.

Yes, you may be feeling small, or dispossessed. But the feeling is temporary. Give yourself time for you to recover from the shock, *resource yourself* and reclaim your powers. Breathe deeply and visualise what you want to happen, rather than what you don't want to happen. You want them all to clear out. You may imagine your teenager and his or her friends calmly clearing up the mess and then departing. Practise making an assertive statement, beginning with 'I'. ('I'd like you to clear up and go home now, please.') When you feel ready to reassert yourself in your own home:

- *Return to the scene.* They might have all vanished anyway. If they're still there, address your assertive remark, in a casual but firm tone, directly to your teenager. 'Terry, I need some space, and I'd like you and your friends to start clearing up now.' This may evoke one of the following responses:

1) If you get a positive response (which is possible) like 'OK, Mum', just say 'Thanks' and remove yourself again. Stay in the vicinity only if you're absolutely sure you can remain in neutral or a very low gear.

2) If you just get a grunt, or words muttered under the breath, say, 'I didn't catch that. Can you give me a sign that you heard me clearly?' (This at least may get a laugh from one or two of the friends, thus engaging their attention.) If your teenager acknowledges your remark, by whatever means or however reluctantly, say 'OK, thanks' and proceed as in point one above.

3) If there is still no response, however, say, 'I don't like being ignored when I'm talking to you,' and proceed to go up a gear. Clearly repeat your original request: 'I need some space, and I'd like you and your friends to start clearing up now.' Move in closer to your teenager, maintaining eye contact and holding your ground. If you now get a response, say 'OK, thanks' and proceed as above.

4) If your teenager continues to ignore you, the chances are that by now one or two of his or her friends will have responded to your request

and will be demonstrating a willingness to cooperate. If so, say 'Thanks' to the friends, move down a gear again and leave *them* to sort out the mess (and your teenager).

5) If you are directly challenged by your teenager – that is, if she or he confronts you or swears at you or refuses to cooperate – stay calm. Slow down, stay on course, drop down a gear and calmly and firmly repeat your request. If the response then is apoplexy or a torrent of abuse, go into neutral until the response subsides, then repeat your request again. You may have to negotiate; staying in a low gear will increase your manoeuvrability. With a bit of flexibility on your part, you and your teenager may be able to agree on some conditions – for example, that the clearing up will happen after the TV programme/video/computer game. Agree a time when the clearing up will be done by. Again, trust that the common sense of the friends will prevail.

- *Remove yourself again*. Go and do something for yourself – have another cup of tea or glass of wine/have a bath/take a walk/phone a friend. It's important that you stay relaxed: you're still in the marathon, or rally, and even if you can't fully enjoy yourself, it's necessary to pace yourself. After the agreed time (approximately):

- *Return to the scene*. If the place has been cleared up (which is possible), you can express your appreciation to your teenager (and friends) and congratulate yourself. If it's still in the process of being tidied, acknowledge that there has been progress and remove yourself again. Make sure you return to check progress.

- *If nothing has happened, go into first gear.* Make an assertive 'I' statement (rather than an accusation) – for example, 'I was expecting you to tidy up in here and you haven't. I'm really annoyed. I'd like it cleared up in the next ten minutes. OK?' Make sure you get agreement, and preferably see some action. You could even make threats: 'If you don't, I'll turn off the TV/video/stereo anyway.' Remove yourself again and return after the agreed time. If still nothing has happened, you have the right to pull the plug on the TV, video, stereo and/or computer. If, however, there are the beginnings of some action, you may want to give them longer/one last chance. (They may have been internally processing your request and making the psychological adjustment.) Remove yourself again, and return to check progress.

- *Reclaim your space.* In the unlikely event that still nothing has happened, it's time to reclaim your space. Stand, with all your power, in the middle of the room until the last person has gone. Pull all the plugs if necessary.

- *It may be that by now you no longer care, anyway.* If it genuinely doesn't seem a problem any more, and you've decided to go out for the evening to enjoy yourself, letting go may be the best solution of all. Insist that the place is cleared up before you go.

  Note: removing yourself does not mean avoiding an issue but using an effective method to steer yourself through it. Here is a summary of 'going through the gears':

REMOVE YOURSELF
RECOGNISE YOUR NEEDS
REHEARSE YOUR STATEMENT
RETURN TO THE SCENE
RECLAIM YOUR POWER
REPEAT YOUR REQUEST
NEGOTIATE IF NECESSARY
REMOVE YOURSELF
RETURN TO THE SCENE
REASSERT YOUR REQUEST
GIVE ULTIMATUM IF NECESSARY
REMOVE YOURSELF
RETURN TO THE SCENE
RECLAIM YOUR SPACE

As you become more practised in the art of changing gears, the whole process becomes smoother and can take a matter of minutes. You may even become adept at removing yourself – detaching – without even leaving the room.

HELPING YOUNG PEOPLE HANDLE CONFLICT

One of the most common forms of conflict in any family is quarrelling between brothers and sisters, often known as 'sibling rivalry'. This may have been going on for years, of course, since teenagers were children; however, they're bigger now and capable of doing more damage. Also, the way you used to handle the problem may no longer be effective.

SIBLING RIVALRY

As a parent, you can use various strategies to help your teenager, and younger children, deal with family quarrels:

- *Let them sort it out.* Avoid taking sides or being involved in any way. Leave responsibility with the young people for sorting out their own problems. It can prevent children falling into familiar roles of 'persecutor' or 'victim' and dragging you in as the 'rescuer' to complete the triangle. Letting them sort things out can help them (and you) break old patterns.

- *Intervene only if absolutely necessary:* for example, if one person is physically attacking another – although this may not be possible if they are bigger and stronger than you are. This kind of intervention is sometimes known as 'firefighting', for obvious reasons.

- *Remain neutral.* If you decide to intervene, for whatever reason, try to stay detached from the issues being argued against. Our own sibling issues, from when we were children, may be being 'triggered' by those of our children. It helps to be aware of this.

- *Ask, 'What's going on?'* Ask them to state clearly what is happening, or state clearly what you *see* happening. For example, 'I see two people looking very angry and upset.'

- *Ask, 'How are you going to sort this out?'* Having identified the problem, remember it's *their* problem. You are still leaving responsibility with them, while at the same time giving them an opportunity to talk about it.

- *Take quarrels seriously.* Arguments can be very irritating, especially if they happen frequently, but it's better to listen than simply to ignore them. However, if your children argue about everything, all the time, you may have to work hard to help them break the pattern. (A parenting course might help – see 'Useful Addresses', page 141.)

Sometimes quarrels between parents and teenager can arise out of a kind of sibling rivalry: if a parent is unwittingly competing with her or his teenager, especially if of the same gender. For example, a mother might always be trying to outdo her daughter in fashion, causing resentment in the daughter, or a father might resent being outsmarted by his son and will constantly try to put him down.

BULLYING

Another form of conflict faced by many teenagers is bullying. Bullying tends to be more prevalent in secondary schools than in primary schools. Not all bullying takes place at school, however. If you are worried that your son or daughter is being bullied, broach the subject with him or her. Although the issue can be a very distressing one, try to remain calm. Even if your teenager doesn't want to talk about the problem, it's important for him or her to know that you consider bullying totally unacceptable behaviour and that action needs to be taken to stop it.

Bullying can be verbal and psychological as well as physical, and can cause serious damage to a young person's confidence and self-esteem. Even though teenagers might want to sort things out without your intervention, it is vital for them to know that you are behind them and that help is available if they want it – either through the school's anti-bullying policy (if effective) or through a telephone helpline. (See 'Useful Addresses', page 141.) Never suggest that she or he 'learns to fight back'. Bullying is a complex problem that may require action on your part (such as contacting the school or, in cases of community bullying, the police) to overcome it.

If you are worried that your son or daughter may be bullying others, talk to him or her about it and let him or her know that you consider bullying absolutely unacceptable behaviour. Then listen to his or her side of the story and support him or her if necessary in changing his or her behaviour. Bullying is often a symptom of distress or low self-esteem. Try talking with your teenager about what could be some of the underlying reasons.

You will probably need to devote extra time and energy to your teenager at this time. She or he may need additional help as well, perhaps from a counsellor or an educational psychologist. (See 'Useful Addresses'.)

WHAT TO DO WHEN YOU'RE GETTING NOWHERE

If, in conflict with your teenager, you've gone past the point of negotiation or effective communication, you may have to consider other options. For example:

• *Hold peace talks.* Arrange a mutually convenient

time and place and bring in a third party. This could be a friend or relative deemed by you *and* your teenager to be impartial. This person's role would be to observe rather than to intervene. Sometimes, having a 'neutral' person present can help both sides communicate in a relatively civilised way.

- *Appoint a mentor.* It may be that you are not the best person for your teenager to talk to. He or she may prefer to turn to someone else for advice and support. You may need a mentor or a counsellor for yourself as well.
- *Mediation.* Mediation could be arranged informally, through a friend who agreed to take that role, or you could contact family mediation services. (See 'Useful Addresses', page 141.)
- *Family therapy.* Often, a conflict involves more than one family member. All relationships are intertwined, anyway, and family therapy is a supportive way of disentangling conflict and of understanding the deeper issues.

Chapter Six
COPING WITH EMOTIONS

HANDLE WITH CARE

Hormonal turmoil and emotional development – not to mention the ups and downs of life – all contribute to teenagers feeling a range of very powerful emotions. They do not always show their emotions, however. If they do, sometimes their outbursts and mood swings can lead to a rollercoaster ride of family life. In addition, the process of transition from child to adult involves separation from the parent, which in itself can lead to deep, hidden feelings of pain and loss. Parents, too, may be coping with their own feelings of separation and loss. The teenage years can be an emotionally fraught time for parents and teenagers.

Possibly one of the reasons smoking is still popular among teenagers (and adults) is that, quite apart from the so-called glamorous images of cigarette advertising, smoking tobacco helps to keep feelings down. Tobacco suppresses emotion; therefore it is no wonder that it is used so often as a prop. Teenagers may use it as a survival strategy.

But suppressing emotions is not healthy. Emotions give our life energy and meaning. Prolonged denial of emotions can be mentally and physically damaging. A teenager whose feelings are denied constantly is at risk of being depressed or of developing antisocial behaviour.

To care for your own wellbeing and the wellbeing of your teenager, it's important to create a home environment where emotions are permissible. That doesn't mean all family members going round throwing 'wobblies' every five minutes; what it means is every family member being entitled to feel happy or angry or sad, or whatever she or he is feeling *at any time*, without being judged that he or she 'shouldn't' be feeling that way. It means being able to communicate about emotions and accept emotions in others. This is what is known as 'emotional intelligence'.

Sometimes, just acknowledging what a teenager is feeling can help him or her to cope with quite difficult emotions. For example, if your daughter says she is worried about going to school, an unhelpful response might be to say, 'Don't be silly, there's nothing to worry about.' This would probably cause her to worry more and to feel unsupported. A helpful response, on the other hand, might be to say, simply, 'You're worried?' This acknowledges the emotion, also making possible a conversation: the daughter might go on to say something like, 'Yes, there's been some bullying going on, and I'm worried they're going to pick on me.'

Talking about feelings can be the key to understanding. It is also a way of providing emotional support. Equally supportive can be simply respecting what teenagers are feeling *without* the need to talk about it. That is, to leave them alone with the privacy of their feeling, without asking intrusive questions or trying to make them feel better. That is not your role. You are doing them more of a favour by *accepting* their feelings of hurt or discontent or whatever, and letting them be. Teenagers need to be given space in which to learn how to cope with their own emotions.

THE VALUE OF FEELINGS

Just as physical sensations help keep us alive, so do emotional ones. A child whose fingers get burned learns to stay away from the fire. A teenager who feels emotional pain learns about who or what is dear to him or her.

Emotions, like physical feelings, keep us in touch with our needs. If my stomach's rumbling, I'm hungry, therefore I need to eat. If I'm feeling frightened, I need to defend or protect myself, and so on. Emotions, anyway, are often experienced as physical sensations in the body: butterflies in the stomach, for example, when nervous, or burning with anger.

Sometimes you may feel a conflict of emotions in relation to your teenager: hence the love-hate syndrome, which is usually reciprocated. Or you may feel infuriated that while you're coping with so much responsibility and stress, she or he is acting as if life's a joke, as if she/he doesn't have a care in the world. If you're feeling this way, stay in touch with the feeling. It's a way of putting you in touch with your needs. Stop, and instead of focusing on the negative aspects of your teenager, ask yourself: *What do I need?* Tune in to your body. If your body feels tense, maybe you need a luxurious soak in the bath or a massage.

Often we're so busy that we're not really feeling all our feelings. Maybe if we stopped and tuned in to our emotions we'd find we had almost as broad a range of ups and downs as our teenagers. Often these feelings are so painful that it's easier to avoid them. Opening up to our feelings helps us be more open to others, including our teenagers.

Emotions are part of the fertile ground of life which helps us to grow (whether we're an adult or a teenager). Negative or painful feelings are as much a part of life as any other emotion or physical sensation. They are not just something to be 'endured'; more something to be fully savoured and digested or 'processed'. They help us learn and handle life's situations. Helping teenagers learn to value and deal with their feelings will help them handle all kinds of experiences and crises and will give them a positive grounding in life.

Being in touch with feelings also helps to develop intimacy and build positive relationships.

COMMUNICATING ABOUT FEELINGS

Often it's easier to *experience* our feelings than put them into words. This means it can be hard to know what our teenagers are feeling, or indeed, for us to express what *we're* feeling. Body language often reveals feelings, however, as does tone of voice or mood. Sometimes, if a feeling is unexpressed, it may spill out in other ways. For example, a youngster who is full of hurt and resentment may resort to bullying or other antisocial behaviour.

Developing the habit of talking about your own feelings is a healthy move that will make it easier for your teenager to talk about his or her feelings as well. Practise doing so at times when neither you nor your teenager is overwhelmed by emotions – for example, saying, 'I feel really frustrated that I can't get the video to work,' or 'You seem to be feeling a bit low this morning.'

When communicating about your own feelings, it's important to say, 'I feel . . . sad/hurt/angry,' and not 'You make me feel . . . sad/hurt/angry.' This is known as 'owning' your feelings: you are responsible for your own emotion and not making it the other person's fault. Whatever the *behaviour* of the other person that may have caused you to feel that way, your emotion is *your* emotion. In the same way, teenagers need to learn to take responsibility for *their* emotions.

The more you share and support expression of emotions in your teenager, the more you and she or he will understand each other, and the more she or he will learn to deal with strong emotion. Never expect your teenager to bare all his or her feelings, however; always respect his or her right to privacy. Some emotional states are too complex or painful to talk about anyway. Sometimes mental and emotional states are better expressed through music, art or poetry.

Here is a poem expressing the volcanic state of a thirteen-year-old girl:

IT HAS NO MERCY

It has no mercy,

Destroying that which lies in its way

Feeding from the innocent's pain
It cuts too deep to heal again
Fight or not your life will decay;

It has no mercy,
Yet, it lets you rest and start again
It gives you time to reach the top
Then running like the devil's blood it will not stop
There's no escape, nothing seems sane;

It has no mercy,
The mountain from where it flows is unlocked
with a twisted key
Like savage dogs the boiling rocks unleashed
On your life it will feast
And if you survive you'll look back and
think, why me?

HELPING A CHILD OR TEENAGER WHO IS UPSET

One of the most valuable ways of helping children or teenagers who are upset is to be available to listen, if they want to talk – or to let them have a good cry if they need to. Even if they don't want to talk about whatever it is that is upsetting them, the fact that they know you are available and empathic can help them feel supported. The best way of letting them know that you care is to develop the listening habit, and not just when they are upset. That way they know that, if they want to communicate, the door is open.

It's important to differentiate between 'empathy'

and 'sympathy'. *Sympathy* tends to imply that you feel sorry for someone, that in some way she or he is helpless or in a situation of feeling powerless. *Empathy*, on the other hand, suggests you *feel for* the other person without feeling sorry for him or her. Sympathy has an element of pity in it, whereas empathy is empowering.

If you want your teenager to be able to handle his or her emotions, it's vital to let him or her be responsible for his or her emotions. That means respecting what she or he is feeling in any given moment *without judging or criticising*. It means being able to help your teenager find his or her solutions to a problem without feeling the need to fix it for him or her. Our role, as parents, is not to try to make things better but to empower our teenagers to make things better for themselves and to work through problems.

Depending on your style of parenting, you may be a parent who distances yourself, or overreacts to your teenager's problems. Here are some suggestions on how to be actively supportive without interfering:

- *Accept feelings.* If a teenager is sad, upset or angry, *accept* that she or he is sad, upset or angry. Do not attempt to *change* the feeling. She or he is responsible for doing that for herself or himself.
- *Acknowledge feelings.* If a teenager is sad, upset or angry, say, 'You seem sad/upset/angry.' This lets her or him know that you *know* she or he is sad/upset/angry. It shows your acceptance of what she or he is feeling and makes it easier to communicate about it. It gives the teenager the chance to say, 'No, I'm not upset,' or 'Of course

I'm angry.' It also helps her or him accept her or his own feelings.

- *Accept it as their problem.* If your teenager doesn't want to talk about her or his problem, respect his or her right not to do so. More often than not, teenagers sort out their own problems (with or without the support of their friends). Moreover, if you successfully detach yourself from their problem, they are more likely to feel able to discuss it with you. (Try to avoid having any expectations, however.)

- *Allow time.* If a teenager is sad, upset or angry, it's likely that she or he will be feeling *too* sad, upset or angry to talk about things right at that moment. Having acknowledged the feelings, it may be helpful to say, 'Well, let me know if you want to talk about it later.'

- *Affirm choices.* When and if your teenager describes a particular problem, it is helpful to listen to his or her view of the situation and then help him or her to recognise the choices available in how to respond to the situation. Discuss the matter and help her or him to explore what options are open. This will help to empower your teenager to make sensible decisions and feel supported in the process of doing so.

- *Ask open questions.* It is more helpful to ask open questions, such as 'How can I help?' or 'What's going on?', than closed questions, such as 'Did he hit you?', which allow only 'Yes' or 'No' as the answer.

- *Avoid 'dumping'.* When a teenager is upset, it can

be easy for us as parents to get upset as well, and to 'dump' our feelings on our teenager. For example, 'I *told* you he was a no-good, thieving drop-out' or (the classic) 'It's your own fault; you've only got yourself to blame.' This is not helpful to your teenager. What is more helpful is to detach yourself from the issue as much as possible (that is, *to remain in neutral*) and be responsible for your own feelings – for example, 'I'm sad to see you so upset,' or 'I feel frustrated that I can't do anything to help you.'

- *Take issues seriously.* If your teenager is very upset about a seemingly trivial problem, the fact that he or she is so upset suggests that the problem is serious for him or her. It is also possible that there is a more serious problem underneath. For example, if Kevin seems to overreact because his older brother teases him, perhaps the thing that's really upsetting him is that he's been the victim of bullying at school.

- *Seek outside help if necessary.* If your teenager is upset about a serious issue, such as bullying or racial or sexual harassment (verbal or otherwise), it is vitally important that you and he or she decide together on what action needs to be taken to address the problem. Your teenager needs to know that a course of action is available for this particular problem and that there are outside lines of support. This way, she or he learns that she or he can seek outside help in dealing with problems.

This may involve speaking or writing to the school authorities (teacher, headteacher or school governors). It may involve contacting the police, or the Council for Community Relations. In addition many excellent helplines offer advice and guidance on specific problems. (See 'Useful Addresses', page 141.)

If your child or teenager seems inconsolable, or if she or he seems very depressed or disturbed, it is wise to visit your family doctor, who may refer her or him to counselling or child guidance.

DEALING WITH GRIEF

If there has been bereavement in the family, or a divorce or separation, there are probably strong feelings of grief and other emotions. There could be a whole mixture of emotions, from anger to emptiness to despair. Emotions may or may not be shown outwardly; sometimes the process is inward, and sometimes a person will simply feel numb. Allow yourself and your teenager time to process these feelings, and be as gentle on each other as possible. It helps if you can talk about what you're feeling. Coping with loss is never easy, and you may want to seek support for yourself through counselling or bereavement counselling. (See 'Useful Addresses'.)

DEALING WITH ANGER

Anger is one of the most difficult emotions to deal with in other people. It can be a violent emotion, with the power to hurt others or to cause damage to property. The wrath of teenagers can be particularly alarming, especially as they were a lot smaller and younger not so long ago.

However, anger is also a useful and healthy emotion that serves many purposes:

- It connects us to our root feelings and needs.
- It alerts us to threats or danger and helps us to protect ourselves.
- It alerts us to the fact that something needs to change and that action needs to be taken.
- It helps us identify what needs to happen.
- It gives us the power and energy to act.

Anger itself, like any emotion, is energy, which is neutral. It is how we deal with, or express anger which makes it a positive or negative experience. The more we learn to handle our own anger, the more we are able to help our teenagers handle theirs. And the more 'comfortable' we are with our own anger, the more we are able to handle it in others. Here are some points to practise:

- *Own your anger.* Your anger is your own. Say 'I'm angry' rather than 'You stupid, mindless oaf.' Although it's easy to blame or shame someone, or 'dump' our feelings on someone when we're feeling angry, it is better to 'own' our anger. Being able to say (or scream or yell) 'I'm furious' is clean and clear. It is a short, sharp (razor-sharp) declaration of anger which cuts through any crap. It is like a swift arrow fired into the air. Clean anger gets results, and no one is hurt as a consequence. Once expressed, it is over very quickly. And your teenager (or anyone else, for that matter) is likely to sit up and take note.

- *Change the range.* Anger covers a broad range of emotions, from 'mildly irritated' at one end of the spectrum to 'murderous rage' at the other. Next time you feel angry, or cross or annoyed, notice your position within the range, and use appropriate words to describe how you feel – for example, 'I'm feeling annoyed' or 'I'm very cross' or *'I'm really bloody angry!'*

  As you become more aware of your own range, it becomes easier to say what you're feeling angry or annoyed about, before it has the chance to build up into full-blown fury.

- *Say why you're angry.* Having declared your anger and said, 'I'm a bit fed up' or 'extremely annoyed', etc, explain what you are angry about: 'I'm angry *because . . . '* Then *state what you want to happen.* For example, 'I'm fed up with always having to pick up your dirty socks. *What I want* is for you to put away your own dirty washing.' Often the force of the anger, *together with* the assertive statement, has the desired effect.

  It may be something your teenager has done that has made you feel angry. Or, although that might have been a contributing factor, it may be your anger has been triggered because of being under stress. In these circumstances it is more helpful to say to your teenager, 'Sorry, I've been under a lot of pressure at work this week,' than to make her or him responsible for your anger.

- *Acknowledge needs.* Often anger is a result of needs not being met. Ask yourself, 'What do I need?' You may be feeling hungry/tired/thirsty. If so, it's important to identify and see to your needs. Your needs may be longer term – for example, the need for emotional support or security, or the need for time to work through your own emotional issues. If so, focus your energy on taking care of yourself and meeting those needs rather than on blaming your teenager and giving her or him a hard time unnecessarily. Working with your anger, rather than being a victim – or making others a victim – of it, can produce miraculous results. Using anger as a powerful communication tool rather than as a weapon means you have more control over it. It helps to express anger early on rather than wait for a massive build-up. There are also many ways of preventing an accumulation of anger. For example, dancing, running, yoga, meditation, swimming or massage all help to relieve tension.

DEALING WITH AN ANGRY TEENAGER

Often, anger is a symptom of a teenager being upset in some way, and usually the best response is to deal with it in the same way as we would a teenager who was upset. In other words:

- *Acknowledge the feelings:* for example, 'I know you're angry. I know you're upset.' This is not always easy, especially if you're feeling angry and upset yourself. But, if you can manage to take a deep breath and detach (*go into neutral*) for a moment, you may help the anger subside. It may flare up for a while, at first, but then, having been given the chance of an 'airing', it is more likely to extinguish itself than if you had given the message 'Don't be angry.'

- *Acknowledge the need:* 'I know you need a new pair of shoes, and I'm sorry you can't have them this month.'
- *Don't take it personally.* Even though your teenager's anger may be directed towards you, try to avoid taking it 'on board'. Remember it is *his* or *her* anger. Try to remain calm.

  If you're angry as well, *say so*. But meeting anger with more anger can be counterproductive. And just as *you* may express anger as a result of being under pressure, your teenager's anger may also be an eruption, a symptom of being under pressure. Sometimes anger is best left to burn itself out.
- *Talk and listen.* You may have to wait and talk after your teenager has calmed down. Listen to his or her reasons for feeling angry. There are probably issues that you and he or she need to address, which the anger has brought to a head.
- *Identify needs.* Anger can be a result of unmet needs. Your teenager may be hungry/tired/thirsty etc. Often, once the need is identified and met, the anger goes away.

  There may be a deeper, unidentified need leading to your teenager's anger, although she or he may not admit it. She or he may be struggling with a subject at school, for example, and may be needing help. She or he may have a difficulty through dyslexia or problems with literacy or numeracy. These can lead to enormous amounts of frustration and anger, especially if adequate support is not forthcoming. It's important to monitor your teenager's needs. If he or she is not satisfied, or you are not satisfied that these needs are being met, action needs to be taken.

- *Safety first.* Because anger, like fire, is a volatile and dangerous thing, you may have to take safety precautions. Obviously, if your teenager is in an uncontrollable rage and coming towards you with a knife, you should get out of the way and leave the house if necessary.

  Your teenager's safety is also important. If you think she or he is at risk of doing harm to her- or himself, seek help or do what you reasonably can to provide some safety. For example, if she or he is thumping a fist on the table, say calmly, 'Here's a cushion. I suggest you thump that instead.'

- *Anger not aggression.* Let your teenager know that anger is acceptable, whereas aggressive behaviour is not. She or he may need to learn the difference between anger and aggression. The more effectively you manage your own anger, the more of an example you set her or him to follow.

DEALING WITH A TEENAGER'S TANTRUM

A tantrum is anger out of control. Dealing with a tantrum in a toddler can be a distressing enough experience; in a teenager it can be even more alarming. The parent may have the same feelings of helplessness, with the added problem of the 'baby' possibly being bigger than the parent now, and with a lot more weight to throw around. And when someone is taken over by a tantrum, his or her energy fills the whole room.

Obviously, there are varying degrees of tantrums, from an outburst of anger to being out of control. Different families have different definitions. And tantrums can be occasional or they can be habitual. Whatever the situation, should *your* teenager go into one, here are some suggestions for how to cope:

- *Try to remain calm.* If a child or teenager has lost his or her temper, it is very easy for the parent to become upset and angry as well. Try to remain in neutral, without engaging in your own or your teenager's emotional issues. If this is not possible, try instead *removing yourself* until the storm subsides.
- *Put safety first.* Being with a teenager who is out of control can be frightening. If you think there is a risk of violence, or of your teenager inflicting self-harm, do what you can to provide for your own and/or your teenager's safety.
- *Use your voice.* Talk to your teenager in a calm tone of voice. Even if she or he has lost control, she or he will still be able to hear you. Even though you may not get a response (other than more screams and wails, perhaps), continue speaking calmly and clearly. Say, for example, 'I can see you are very angry and upset, and I know it can be scary having such strong feelings . . . ' Your voice helps to maintain contact and may have a calming effect, even if the words themselves aren't heeded. Also, by acknowledging the strong feelings, you are communicating empathy while still holding firm.
- *Avoid giving in.* It may be that your teenager

learned very early on, as a child, that throwing a tantrum was an effective method of getting her or his own way. In these cases a tantrum is a form of emotional blackmail. If the behaviour is long-established, it may be harder for you and your teenager to break the pattern. You are probably afraid of her or his tantrums, which gives her or him more power over you. However, with perseverance and the practice of 'detachment' (staying in neutral) you may find it easier to *allow* your teenager to pass through his or her tantrums without giving in to her or him.

You may need to seek some emotional back-up for yourself during this transition. It is worth working on it because, in the long run, *holding your ground is more supportive of your teenager than giving in.* It will help him or her break emotionally manipulative patterns that may otherwise impede him or her in adulthood.

Chapter Seven
COMMUNICATION AND SELF-ESTEEM

CREATING THE RIGHT CONDITIONS

Many of the strategies and skills described throughout this book will help to build confidence and self-esteem in your teenager. For example, by listening to your son or daughter with respect, you are helping him or her to treat himself or herself with respect. Or by setting appropriate boundaries you are helping her or him feel confident in knowing what is acceptable or unacceptable behaviour.

Helping to build your teenager's self-esteem is one of the most effective ways of equipping her or him to grow into a caring, responsible adult. This is as much about *creating favourable conditions* as it is about doing anything specific. And one of the most significant elements in these conditions is, of course, *communication*.

Creating favourable conditions for communication requires commitment and time. And, even though you may not always see short-term 'results', trust that the long-term benefits *are* there.

A teenager with positive self-esteem is more likely to:

- have a positive attitude towards life;
- have a feeling of inner strength;
- be able to stand up for him or herself;
- form positive relationships;
- do well at school and/or in work, and
- be caring and supportive towards others.

Self-esteem will also be influenced by factors outside the home, of course. And self-acceptance is hard if you don't *feel* accepted – if you are struggling with issues of cultural or racial oppression, for example. Or, for girls especially, it can be very hard to have a positive self-image when there are so many commercial and social pressures to *look* a particular way. Many neuroses and eating disorders have their origins in low self-esteem and negative self-image. Keeping in mind what you, as a parent, and your teenager may be up against, you may have to work extra hard at helping to affirm your son or daughter's self-esteem.

AFFIRMING SELF-ESTEEM

- *Take time.* Even with all the pressures of life, taking time to communicate reaps rewards. This doesn't mean allocating 'quality time' (which implies that the rest of time is inferior); it means taking time to *connect* on a regular basis, as part of your daily routine where possible (such as at family mealtimes). It also means being flexible, so that you are able to stop what you are doing *at any time*, if necessary, in order to communicate.

Obviously, this may not always be possible, in which case it is important to say something like, 'I know this is important. Can we make a time to talk about it later?' And then keep to your word.

What matters is that you give communication with your teenager the time it deserves. This will help your son or daughter to feel valued and supported. It will also help to prevent crises because it means issues and problems are addressed properly and in good time. Taking ten minutes to communicate about something *now* may save ten days of trouble later on. As well as helping your teenager's self-esteem, taking time to communicate can *save* time.

- *Show commitment.* Of course you are committed as a parent, otherwise you wouldn't be reading this book. But *showing* commitment is an active demonstration to your teenager that you are committed to her or him. Sometimes, in the role of parent, we are so caught up in worrying about or quarrelling with our teenagers that we forget to let them know *we are on their side.* It helps to remind ourselves, and them, of this sometimes. Helping our teenager know that we support them in what they are doing or, put another way, that we want her or him to 'win', can do a lot for her or his self-confidence.

- *Give appreciation.* A little appreciation can go a long way. Remember to appreciate your son or daughter for something she or he has done, whether it's 'I appreciate you taking the rubbish out this morning,' or 'I appreciate you're really making an effort with your homework.' Best of all is to give appreciation from time to time just for being who they are.

- *Give positive attention.* Attention itself is neutral. However, sometimes just giving some attention to your teenager – whether discussing some homework your son is doing or looking at some computer graphics with your daughter – means giving attention and approval to something positive she or he may have said or done. Many parents give attention only to their teenager's *negative* behaviour which, as well as reinforcing the behaviour, has the effect of reducing, rather than enhancing self-esteem.

- *Give responsibility.* Ask your teenager to help you in tasks around the home or garden which she or he is able to achieve. The feeling of responsibility and *achievement* that this can bring can help her or him feel valued and successful. This is especially important if she or he has been having a difficult time recently or experienced a loss of confidence. Please note, however, that it is *not* helpful to burden your teenager with so much responsibility that she or he is not free to enjoy a relatively normal teenage life.

- *Trust in your teenager's abilities.* Let your son or daughter feel that you have confidence in her or his abilities. You can even say 'I trust in your abilities.' This statement in itself can have a powerful effect in helping a teenager trust in her or his own abilities. If you are too critical, or overprotective, you take away from, rather than enhance your teenager's sense of empowerment.

- *Help your teenager make changes.* If your teenager needs to make changes in her or his behaviour – say, for example, she or he has been in trouble at school or with the police for antisocial behaviour – she or he may need to be given help in learning new behaviour. This can take time, but with your support and empowerment the process can be positive. Discussing the difficulties and setting realistic goals will help your teenager develop self-esteem as well as take responsibility for her- or himself. She or he may also need some extra or outside help at this time.

- *Cultivate emotional security.* By acknowledging our teenagers' feelings we help them feel valued and understood *as people.* By communicating our own feelings as well, we help to create a climate in which it is acceptable to express positive or negative emotion. Even when things are difficult, it is more supportive to say, 'I'm finding this situation really painful,' than to pretend everything is fine.

  Children, teenagers and adults tend to feel more insecure during times of change and transition. This is all the more reason to accept and acknowledge our own and our teenagers' feelings, and to let our teenagers know we care about them. This helps each person feel valued, and builds a sense of emotional security in what is often an insecure world.

Helping build your teenager's self-esteem is a gradual and gentle process. Do not expect instant results (although it is wonderful when they happen). Your son or daughter may continue to sulk or display neurotic behaviour, but self-esteem is an inner quality, and there may have been significant changes that are not at first visible. The best you can do is to continue to communicate a supportive attitude and hope that your positive messages eventually become internalised by your teenager.

THE BENEFITS OF LISTENING

One of the most beneficial ways of helping build your teenager's confidence and self-esteem is to develop the art of listening. We've already looked at the many ways in which listening can be supportive, as well as making communication more effective. Furthermore, the more practised you become, the more your teenager will have confidence in your listening abilities, and the more likely she or he will be willing to *talk*.

In terms of self-esteem, a teenager who has the experience of being listened to in a non-judgemental way is likely to feel:

- respected;
- accepted;
- taken seriously;
- supported;
- understood, and
- valued.

A teenager who feels accepted is more able to make choices in, for example, changing his or her behaviour. Or a teenager who is given the opportunity to talk about feelings and opinions can be helped to listen to her or his own feelings. This helps her or him to respect her or his own needs and to take responsibility. It also fosters an atmosphere of *mutual* support and cooperation. Listening helps them work out solutions to problems and to realise their potential to do so. Listening is *empowering*.

Listening to our teenager with empathy and gentleness helps her or him develop empathy towards others.

THE ART OF LISTENING

Here are some guidelines to enhancing listening:

- *Allow time and space.* Listening can be done at any time. In order to be fully focused, however, it is best done at a time and place where you will not be interrupted. If you have younger children, for example, make an arrangement with your teenager to have 'listening time' with her or him on your own. A relaxed attitude is especially important when listening.

- *Have a clear intention.* It's important for you to be clear about *why* you are listening. If it is purely out of your own need to know things about your teenager, this may be more interrogative than supportive listening. This may be appropriate in certain situations, although we are talking here about *focused* listening, designed for support and open communication.

   If you are hoping for a specific or definite outcome after listening, you may be disappointed. The idea of focused listening is to *listen* to whatever views or feelings the other person may wish to express. If you are clear of your intention to listen and support, without necessarily arriving at a conclusion, you are more likely to help the other person and be heard as well.

- *Be accepting.* Even if you don't *agree* with what your teenager may say or disclose about her or his feelings or behaviour, it's important to listen in as non-judgemental a way as possible. Knowing that he or she has certain feelings or ways of behaving doesn't mean you accept the behaviour. It just means you're fully *listening* to him or her without letting your own beliefs or opinions cloud the issue.

  Being accepting means being able to go into neutral and detach yourself from your own issues. It also means respecting your teenager's space without expecting him or her to volunteer any more information than she or he wants to.

  Your accepting attitude will help build trust between you and your teenager.

- *Give feedback.* Still in accepting mode, give feedback to your teenager to let her or him know you have heard what has been said. This can be done by simple repetition, for example:

TEENAGER: 'School sucks.'
PARENT: 'You don't like school?'
  (This helps the teenager feel heard and opens the door to further communication.)
TEENAGER: 'I *hate* school.'
PARENT: 'You hate it?'
TEENAGER: 'Yeah. Especially the teachers. Well, one teacher in particular.' (*kicks a chair*)

PARENT: 'There's one teacher you don't like.'

TEENAGER: 'Yeah, the one who teaches *maths*.' (*kicks a cushion across the room*)   'Old fat-face – I *hate* him.'

PARENT: 'You don't like him.'

TEENAGER: 'No, I said I *hate* him. He picks on me all the time.'

PARENT: 'He picks on you?'

And so on . . . By feeding back what was being said, the parent helped the teenager to identify a problem. Now they can go on to talk about it, and possibly arrive at a course of action.

STORYTELLING

One of the parental rituals in many households when children are young is to read them a bedtime story. Sadly, this habit tends to disappear as children grow older. The children become more independent and get themselves off to sleep without a story. However, in many of the world's traditions and cultures, story-telling is alive and well *for all ages*, and not just at bed-time. It is a way of interpreting events and passing on myths and legends from one generation to another.

If you can find the time and inclination (and will-power to turn off the television, which is the modern-day equivalent of storytelling) to sit occasionally with friends or members of your family and take it in turns to read or make up a story or two (or read from a mag-azine or newspaper cutting), you may be pleasantly surprised at the positive effect this has on communication with your teenager. (If she or he deigns to be present, that is.) It can lead to all kinds of imaginative interpretations and discussion, and may have a problem-solving element as well.

It is an enjoyable and entertaining family event that can help put other events 'on hold' for a while, as well as helping young, old and teenage members of the family feel included, thus helping to reinforce feelings of self-esteem.

Best of all, occasionally, is to ask your teenager to read *you* a story at bedtime.

TEENAGERS AND YOUNGER CHILDREN

Teenagers play an important role in furthering communication with younger members of the family or, if they have no brothers or sisters, other younger children. Teenagers are a kind of stopgap between children and adults and are capable of giving children positive attention – playing with them and/or talking and listening to them. If they treat a younger child with respect, that child in turn experiences self-respect. There are many other things younger children can learn from them. This, in turn, helps the teenager's self-esteem.

Being given responsibility sometimes (but not all the time) for younger children can help to build a teenager's sense of worth – especially if she or he is paid for it, as in baby-sitting. It can also provide an opportunity for teenagers to show some tenderness and affection, which they may not always be able to do in their tough teenage world, especially if they are not yet at the stage of having a girl- or boyfriend.

Having care of a pet can help in a similar way. Make sure he or she takes responsibility for looking after it.

HELPING TEENAGERS CARE FOR THEMSELVES

Self-esteem is something which never stays still. It tends to fluctuate, like a barometer, from poor to fair to moderate. And, like the weather, it cannot be controlled. However, we can create conditions within our own home which may influence our teenager. Feeling respected and cared for helps to build self-esteem. And a teenager with positive self-esteem is more likely to *want* to care for himself or herself.

As a young person grows in self-esteem, he or she will be able to:

- identify his or her own needs;
- state what those needs are;
- do what she or he has to do to meet those needs, without being dependent on others;
- seek help or guidance from others in meeting needs, if necessary;
- respect himself/herself and others;
- make appropriate choices which do not harm himself/herself or others;
- resist negative peer pressure;
- do what feels right for him or her;
- respect own boundaries as well as those of others;
- pick himself or herself up again from the knocks and bruises of life;
- create loving and supportive friendships and relationships;
- avoid destructive friendships and relationships;

- care for himself or herself;
- develop cooperative behaviour, and
- grow into a caring adult.

All these factors contribute to a person's mental, physical and emotional wellbeing. Note: a growing sense of self-esteem does *not* mean feeling superior to others; it is more about *valuing* oneself and others, whatever the weather, whatever the external events going on.

As well as practising the communication skills and attitudes in this book, you'll help to set your teenager an example in caring for herself or himself by making sure you care for yourself as well.

BUILDING YOUR OWN CONFIDENCE AND SELF-ESTEEM

In order to value and care for yourself, *you* need to be able to identify and meet your own needs. This means:

- creating the right conditions: taking time for yourself;
- showing commitment to your own wellbeing: prioritising your needs;
- appreciating yourself: reminding yourself that you are doing a wonderful job as a parent, in difficult circumstances;
- practising the power of positive thought: try saying affirmations that reprogramme negative beliefs about yourself. For example, 'I am doing the best I can' or 'I hold myself in gentle and loving esteem' instead of telling yourself 'I'm useless';
- trusting your own abilities: listening to your 'inner guide', and

- accepting yourself: give up trying to be perfect and accept yourself as you are.

Your needs may be to pursue a particular hobby or interest, or find avenues of creative self-expression, or train for a particular kind of work. There are many wonderful training and adult-education courses on offer. (Visit your local library or contact a local adult education college for details.) These can all help you feel really good about yourself and raise your confidence and self-esteem.

PARENTING CLASSES

These are worthy of a mention all on their own, because one of their main aims is to help raise confidence and self-esteem *in parents* and support parents in making changes in communication and attitude, and so on. They acknowledge all the experience that parents bring and help parents discuss issues and learn from one another, as well as give practical training and exercises in the kinds of skills discussed in this book. Although a relatively new field, a host of parenting courses is now on offer. There may be one in a town near you. (See 'Useful Addresses', page 141.)

Parents sometimes feel nervous about approaching such a group because a strong element in our culture and conditioning still tells us that as parents we should know what we're doing, and if we need to ask for help, something must be wrong with us and our children, and we have failed somehow in our duty as parents. But the reality is that *most* parents find parenthood quite difficult at times, and often a huge feeling of relief is experienced by many parents in these groups because they realise they are not the only ones to feel the way they do. (For example, it's comforting to know you're not alone in sometimes wanting to throttle your teenager.) The positive experience of a parenting course is equivalent to reading a hundred books on parenting.

MEDITATION

Another significant way of developing self-esteem and confidence, as well as deep compassion for others, is to practise meditation. This is the art of detaching the mind from the trials of everyday life and tuning in to a calm, quiet wisdom.

Some people experience meditation as a spiritual connectedness, others as prayer, others as a technique for relaxation. Meditation exists in cultures throughout the world and is a way of helping to keep body, mind and soul together. Many parents have reported that the daily practice of meditation has helped them stay sane and emotionally whole in the face of pressures and adversity. What's more, many of those same parents also report an improvement in all relationships as a result of meditation. They say it has helped them be calmer in dealing with problems and more trusting of their inner wisdom.

That does not mean, however, that they become super-calm at all times! They continue to be real people with the usual range of feelings and dramas of their own.

Meditation, like most things, is best taught by a qualified instructor. (Visit your local library or adult education college for details.)

Chapter Eight
LETTING GO

TOWARDS FREEDOM

Letting go of parental responsibility for your teenager doesn't happen overnight. It tends to happen bit by bit, over the years, as we struggle to walk the tightrope between freedom and control. Finding the balance between allowing independence and keeping a rein on our teenagers is an art in itself. It helps, sometimes, to practise with small things, as early as possible so that by the time the big things are on us, we – and our teenagers – are more able to handle them.

Here is an example of a parent who went away for a weekend, leaving her son, aged fourteen, to fend for himself:

Rose: 'The first time I went away I was really nervous and felt like phoning home every few hours to check that everything was OK. I was imagining all kinds of terrible things happening. When I got back everything was fine, except he and a friend had been living on pancakes all weekend and the kitchen was a total mess – flour and eggshells and sticky mess all over the place. Next time I went away I made it clear I wanted to find the place as I left it.'

Much depends, of course, on the level of maturity of the teenager. Only you and your teenager can decide whether or not she or he is ready for another layer of responsibility. And even then, it's a case of experimenting, putting things to the test. 'Letting go' does not mean abandoning your teenager; it means letting go with love and care and with adequate provision for her or his safety and wellbeing. It is also advisable, in situations such as the above example, mutually to nominate an 'adult-in-charge' – that is, a neighbour or family friend who you and your teenager trust and who agrees to be on call to help if necessary, and who your teenager agrees to report to when going out or coming in, a kind of 'checking in' and 'checking out' system, in order to provide a boundary for your teenager when she or he is *not* at home.

It's important that teenagers – boys and girls – learn to look after themselves and handle independence *with responsibility*. This is something best learned gradually, long before they eventually leave home. Sometimes it's easier to let go when they are younger than when they reach an age of being irresponsible, possibly with alcohol and/or drugs.

Rose 'I've got no qualms, now, that he can fend for himself and take care of the flat. But now that he's a couple of years older, I'd think twice about going away. Things are more likely to get out of control when there's a crowd of them with alcohol, etc.'

It's true that, with teenage parties, a certain wildness takes over (remember?). But whether or not you allow your teenager to throw a party, or go away and leave her or him for the odd weekend, these are all stages towards her or him gaining independence. Next year or the year after she or he may travel abroad on a student exchange visit or, in another few years, could be backpacking around the world. There are many steps in the long haul towards freedom.

FINDING YOUR OWN FREEDOM

We can help to launch our teenagers' journey, but we cannot accompany them. We are fellow travellers through life and need to continue on our own unique journey. As we help release our teenagers into freedom, we can start to gain a sense of our own freedom too.

The following ideas may help you let go of some anxieties about your teenager and instead turn the focus of attention on yourself:

- *Separate your mood from theirs.* Don't let your mood be dependent on their mood. Having done all that bonding with your child, it's now time to treat her or him as a separate being.
- *Manage your time.* In the busy-ness of life, with schedules and endless lists of things to do, it's easy to overlook your own needs. Make sure you include time for yourself and your personal relationships in your diary. For example, book in some relaxation and/or fitness time, or spend an evening out with your partner or a friend.
- *Seek support if necessary.* You may be going through a harder time than you need to. If you are struggling with a personal crisis and/or

relationship problems, there are many helplines and agencies offering advice and support. (See 'Useful Addresses', page 141.)

- *Get used to change.* To become accustomed to change in your own as well as your teenager's life, practise doing something different every day – even if it's just a small thing to start with, like sleeping on the other side of the bed or holding your cup of tea with the opposite hand. You could shop at a different supermarket or take a different route to work. Not only will this help you adjust to change; it may help you create changes as well. It's also a way of keeping yourself fresh and open to new possibilities.

- *Take control of your life.* If you don't have a job or outside interests, you may find your life feels empty at this point. Concentrate on taking up new interests and rebuilding your confidence. Adult education classes offer a fun and inexpensive way of learning all kinds of things in a friendly and supportive atmosphere.

- *Express yourself.* Earlier, we looked at the value of self-expression in our teenager's development. Now it's time to consider (if you haven't already been doing so) your own outlets for self-expression. For example, joining an art class or walking or gliding club or local history society or taking up a new craft or skill – maybe something you've always dreamed of doing but never got round to or never had the nerve to. As well as enhancing self-expression, this is a good way of meeting like-minded people and making new friends.

There are many other ways of expressing yourself, from the way you dress to the way you decorate your home. Be your own person! One of the advantages of growing older is that you are more free to develop an individual style of your own. (If your teenager doesn't like it, tough!)

- *Regain your youthfulness.* While your teenager is growing into an adult, this is a time when you could be reclaiming some of the positive aspects of your childhood. It is the playful being, the child within us, who has the capacity to help bring joy and wonderment and delight back into our lives.

Our 'inner child' brings healing and helps us lighten up and play. When was the last time you had a good laugh? (Last night? Fine, no problem.) If it seems a long time since you had any fun, you may also need to reconnect with your inner teenager as well. But be careful of this one. Someone in the family has to keep on the rails, and it is more appropriate for you, *as the parent*, to be that person.

As well as making you feel better, these ideas may help relationships with your teenager. By giving *yourself* a break, you may be giving your teenager a break as well.

ASSESSING YOUR ROLE

It can be easier for teenagers to let go of their dependence on their parents – because they're programmed to do so – than it can for parents to let go of the parenting role.

Just as teenagers undertake a quest for identity, so

adults continue to seek identity, and one of the most common identities among adults of any culture is that of being a parent. Of course, once a parent, always a parent: *being a parent is a lifelong process* and continues after teenagers become independent adults and leave home. (Eventually, being a parent may also lead to taking on the role of grandparent.) However, the role of parent, and therefore the identity, diminishes. This can leave many parents going through an identity crisis of their own. Most of us need to be needed and, although often a relief, it can also be extremely painful to realise we're not needed any more.

If you've had a close relationship with your teenager, you may even *resent* his or her not needing you to help sort out problems, etc, any more. It may leave you feeling rejected, out in the cold. These are very real feelings, and it's vital that you *take responsibility for your own feelings* without laying them at the feet of your teenager.

Teenagers are like a ship in full sail and, even though they may still need you as an anchor, this will happen less and less until one day they put down an anchor of their own. Because they're undergoing change in every aspect of their life, pulling on their ropes can be counterproductive and you can end up just pulling against them. Are *you* pulling on the ropes to preserve the status quo? If so, are you doing it for *you* or for them? While the odd tug might be necessary, it is advisable not to try to preserve the old habits of a lifetime; your teenager is on a journey towards establishing lifetime habits of his or her own. You could be fighting a losing battle. As they progress into mid-teens and older, it is probably time for you to change *your* habits as well.

It's best to assess your role *often* during the teenage years. If you wait until your teenager leaves home, when you have no *choice* but to assess your role, you may have a bigger shock coming.

A TIME OF TRANSITION

Stepping out of the parenting role can be scary. Sometimes you stop and it hits you: *what have I done with my life?* You may experience feelings of regret, pain and earth-shattering loss – loss of oneself as well as one's child *and* one's teenager. The transition of growing out of one role and yet not knowing where you're going can lead to insecurity and uncertainty.

Parents, like teenagers, are at a time of transition in their lives. Many are approaching or have reached middle age, or 'the middle years' (which sounds better). This means that many of us are going through our own hormonal changes and all the inner – and external – turmoil that those can bring. It also means coping with our own feelings of grief, separation and loss, which are present during any major life transition. It is likely we may also experience bereavement through the loss of one or both of our own parents.

Often, in the hurly-burly of family life there is very little time or space for a parent to reflect on his or her own personal development. Then, as our children grow up, we may find we have more time and some-times that time can feel like a vacuum. We may not like the feelings we experience when we stop and tune in to them. Or it may be tempting to become so busy with other things that our life is completely filled again and we don't have time to dwell on what we're *feeling*. But, unless we are willing to face up to our feelings of loss, and so on, we may find it harder to move successfully on to the next stage.

Sometimes there is no avoiding the stark contrast: our teenagers are growing up while we're growing 'down'. *They* may seem huge, like giants, making us feel diminished in comparison. They're approaching their prime; we're approaching decline. They're glowing; we're fading. The important thing to remember is that, although physically in decline, your wisdom consciousness and enrichment of life continue to grow. And *facing up to feelings doesn't mean wallowing in them;* it means *accepting* them, feeling them and letting them pass. Then you can start to enjoy life again.

You may have feelings of hurt and resentment: you've worked your butt off all these years for them, and what thanks do you get? It's probably better not to expect any. Then, when and if they show any appreciation, it may be all the sweeter for being a surprise.

PICKING UP THE PIECES

After seventeen or eighteen years of parenthood, you may well feel exhausted, not to mention shell-shocked. Your children may or may not have flown the nest, leaving you feeling like the old frayed carpet on the stairs. You may need time to recover from all the ups and downs, while probably still dealing with the day-to-day issues of other members of the family.

You may need time to process feelings of loss and grief or disorientation. After investing so much energy in your children, you may feel empty at first. Your marriage or relationship may also be going through a ground shift. Allow time and space for working through your changing relationship. (Many couples enjoy a new lease of life after the children have grown up and left home.) Eventually, you will probably feel ready to pick up the pieces again and reclaim something of your home, your sanity and your life. Then it's time to pick up the threads and create new patterns.

You may find you want to become more involved in your local community – the larger 'family' – now that not all your energy is going into your own family. In many cultures, the 'elders' of the community play a key role. Or you may want to help *create* community, through networking or joining others who share a similar concern. Although many communities have been disintegrating, many new ones are being formed.

Incidentally, you might seek comfort from the words of one psychologist, who said that teenagers and children are like cats and dogs: when they're young they're like puppies – loving, playful and loyal to their masters – dependent on their parents, in fact; then, when they're in their teens, they become like cats, independent, huffy and nocturnal; then, during their twenties, something happens and they become canine again, friendly, responsive and pleased to see you.

Even if relationships have broken down between you and your teenager, and she or he has left home under a cloud, there is every possibility that she or he will return one day – maybe in weeks or months or years to come – wanting to make peace and be friends again. In these circumstances, it is best to get on with your own life and make sure you keep the door open.

TOWARDS CITIZENSHIP

However much we encourage or empower our teenager, it's a sad fact of life that, in our society, young people are not given much of a voice. When not in the institutions of school or family, children and teenagers are often still marginalised, and we still seem a long way behind our European cousins in integrating them more fully into the community. When given attention (through the media) it is usually because they have got into trouble in some way. Boys, especially, receive an extremely negative press, and girls are still under pressure to conform to social and commercial expectations of how they should *look*. Society is then surprised when teenagers become *more* disruptive or depressed.

It can be hard for parents to encourage their teenagers to be responsible in a climate in which teenagers are not encouraged to take responsibility. Young people are rarely consulted on community, social, political, economic or educational issues. Isn't it strange that society wants them to be more responsible citizens and yet is not willing to take them seriously or listen to them or give them responsibility until they are old enough to vote, at the age of eighteen?

Young people have unlimited talent, enthusiasm, drive and potential. Shouldn't society be taking more notice of them and giving them some positive attention? The rewards for all of us would be far-reaching.

LETTING GO

Our children/teenagers are the young people coming
of age in the new millennium – they are the next generation, the adults of the future. It's a recurring theme,
of course. No wonder society finds them threatening:

The teenagers are coming –
the tide is rushing in,
filling the street
with a roar
of yells and laughter,
a squall,
a squabble
cacophony of sound,
going up a level
beyond the Plimsoll line
(they're wearing trainers)
flooding the sanctity
of staidness,
splashing buildings,
monuments –
claiming their rightful space.
Exciting, terrifying,
no point standing in their way.

It's quiet,
they've gone
until another day.
They'll be back
again and again,
corroding,
slowly eroding
until, with the flotsam and jetsam
they've washed us all away.

APPENDICES

RECOMMENDED BOOKS

Available from Piccadilly Press:
Elliot, Pat: *Coping With Loss for Parents*
         (Piccadilly Press, 1997)
Gillham, Bill (Dr): *Child Safety for Parents*
         (Piccadilly Press, 1996)
Munro, Sheila: *Overcome Bullying for Parents*
         (Piccadilly Press, 1997)
Russell, Adrian & Rosemary: *Information Technology*
         for Parents (Piccadilly Press, 1996)

Floodlight (available at newsagents) – information on
adult education courses in London. (For other areas,
check your local education authority for details.)

Available through Parent Network:
Biddulph, Steve: *Raising Boys*   (Thorsons, 1998)
Pipher, Mary: *Reviving Ophelia*   (Vermilion, 1996)

Booklets and audio cassettes:
Teenagers and Alcohol
Teenagers and Divorce
Teenagers and Drugs
Teenagers and Sexuality
Teenagers and Step-parents
Teenagers – Suicide and self-harm
Teenagers Under Stress
available from the Trust for the Study of Adolescents,
23 New Road, Brighton, East Sussex BN1 1WZ
Tel. 01273 693311

Useful Addresses and Helplines

1. Advisory Centre for Education (ACE)
    22 Highbury Grove, London N5 2DQ
    Tel. 0171 354 8321 (*Advice and information on education*)

2. British Association for Counselling
    1 Regent Place, Rugby CV21 2PJ
    Tel. 01788 578328 (*Information line for details of local counsellors*)

3. British Dyslexia Association
    Helpline: 0118 9668271

4. Brook Advisory Centres,
    Young People's Information line: 0171 713 9000
    (*Information and advice on contraception etc.*)

5. Childline
    Tel. 0800 1111 or write (remembering to include your address)
    to: Freepost 1111, London N1 OBR
    (*A confidential 24-hour helpline for children and teenagers*)

6. The Children's Legal Centre
    Advice line: 01206 873820

7. Commission for Racial Equality (CRE)
    Elliot House, 10-12 Allington Street, London SW1E 5HE
    Tel. 0171 828 7022

8. Eating Disorders Association
    First Floor, Wensum House, 103 Prince of Wales Road
    Norwich NR1 1TW
    Tel. 01603 621414

9. Education Otherwise
    Tel. 0891 518303 (*Advice and information on education at home*)

10. Families Need Fathers
    Helpline 0181 886 0970 (*Advice and support to fathers,
    particularly non-custodials) in maintaining a sound parent/child
    relationship in divorce/separation*)

11. Gingerbread (*National organisation for lone parents*)
    Advicelines: England – 0171 336 8183, Scotland – 0141 353 0953
    Northern Ireland – 01232 234568, Wales – 01792 648728

12. MIND (National Association for Mental Health)
    Tel. 0181 522 1728 (*Advice and free publications on mental health*)
    (See also: Young Minds)

13. National AIDS Helpline
    0800 567 123 (*24-hour advice and information line on* HIV and
    AIDS)

14. National Association of Bereavement Services
    20 Norton Folgate, London E1 6DB
    Tel. 0171 247 1080

15. National Council for the Divorced and Separated
    Tel: 0116 2700 595

16. National Drugs Helpline
    0800 776600

17. National Family Mediation
    9 Tavistock Place, London WC1H 9SN
    Tel. 0171 383 5993

18. National Stepfamily Association
    3rd Floor, Chapel House, 18 Hatton Place, London EC1N 8RU
    Tel. 0171 209 2460 (*Publications and advice for members of
    stepfamilies*)

19. NSPCC (National Society for the Prevention of Cruelty to Children) Child Protection Helpline: 0800 800500 (24 hours)

20. Parentline
    Tel. 01702 559900 (*National helpline for parents*)

21. Parent Network
    2 Winchester House, 11 Cranmer Road, London SW9 1EJ
    Tel. 0171 735 1214 (*Details of parenting courses in England, Scotland & Wales*)

22. Relate National Marriage Guidance
    Herbert Gray College, Little Church Street, Rugby CV21 3AP
    01788 573241

23. Re-Solv
    Tel. 01785 817885 (*Information and advice on substance abuse*)

24. The Samaritans
    Tel. 0345 909090 (*24-hour helpline for suicidal or despairing people*)

25. Trust for the Study of Adolescence
    Tel. 01273 693311 (*Advice and publications for parents and adolescents*)

26. United Kingdom Advocacy Network
    14–18 West Bar Green, Sheffield S1 2DA
    0114 272 8171

27. Young Minds
    Tel. 0345 626376 (*Helpline for young people on mental or emotional issues*)

28. Youth Access
    Tel. 0181 772 9900 (*Provides names of local youth counsellors*)

INDEX